READING
KARL BARTH

READING KARL BARTH

Theology That Cuts Both Ways

CHRIS BOESEL

Rusty, you were there at the beginning of my theological journey. Thanks for making space for us misfits to find our way!

CASCADE Books · Eugene, Oregon

READING KARL BARTH
Theology That Cuts Both Ways

Copyright © 2023 Chris Boesel. All rights reserved. Except for brief quotations in critical publications or reviews, no part of this book may be reproduced in any manner without prior written permission from the publisher. Write: Permissions, Wipf and Stock Publishers, 199 W. 8th Ave., Suite 3, Eugene, OR 97401.

Cascade Books
An Imprint of Wipf and Stock Publishers
199 W. 8th Ave., Suite 3
Eugene, OR 97401

www.wipfandstock.com

PAPERBACK ISBN: 978-1-4982-0034-9
HARDCOVER ISBN: 978-1-4982-8502-5
EBOOK ISBN: 978-1-4982-0035-6

Cataloguing-in-Publication data:

Names: Boesel, Chris, author.
Title: Reading Karl Barth : theology that cuts both ways / Chris Boesel.
Description: Eugene, OR : Cascade Books, 2023 | Includes bibliographical references.
Identifiers: ISBN 978-1-4982-0034-9 (paperback) | ISBN 978-1-4982-8502-5 (hardcover) | ISBN 978-1-4982-0035-6 (ebook)
Subjects: LCSH: Barth, Karl, 1886–1968. Kirchliche Dogmatik. | Theology, Doctrinal.
Classification: BT75.B286 B64 2023 (paperback) | BT75.B286 B64 (ebook)

VERSION NUMBER 12/27/22

For John Linton and Doug Frank, who first led me to accept Karl Barth into my heart as my personal lord and savior; and for Kait Dugan, who may yet save Barth scholarship from the citadel of straight white dudes like me

CONTENTS

Acknowledgments • ix

Introduction • xi

PART 1: **Approaching Barth's Theology—What Is Theology about and What Is at Stake?**

1 I've Got One Word for You: Jesus Christ • 3

2 The News Is Good: God Is *for* Us, Period • 15

PART 2: **The Method, Logic, and Content of Barth's Theology—How Are We Supposed to *Do* Theology and What Should It *Say* (and *Not* Say)?**

3 Neither Our Possession nor at Our Disposal: The Break with Liberal Theology, the Turn to the Bible, and Encountering an Unknown God • 29

4 The Movement of Barth's Theological Logic—*from God* • 51

5 The Concreteness of Barth's Theological Logic—*Only* in Jesus Christ • 77

PART 3: **The Ethics of Barth's Theology—"How Should We Then Live?"**

6 We Do Stuff Too: Human Agency, Freedom, and Action • 103

7 Barth and Progressive Christian Ethics in and for Our Time and Place? • 125

Bibliography • 151

ACKNOWLEDGMENTS

Special thanks are due to Kait Dugan for giving me the nod for this project; to John Linton, Doug Frank, and the Oregon Extension community circa the mid-1980s, for introducing me to Barth when I desperately needed the kind of theological alternative to conservative evangelicalism that he opened up for me; to my gifted research assistant, Min Um, for all the hours in the library helping to ensure that what I write in these pages is not entirely out in left field vis-à-vis Barth scholarship; and to my mom and dad, for arguing with me about Barth for thirty-five years and never giving up on the argument.

INTRODUCTION

AUDIENCE, GOALS, AND SCOPE

THIS INTRODUCTION TO THE theology of Karl Barth is intended as a guide for theologically invested readers interested in serious engagement with Barth's work, for either personal or vocational reasons. Its general goal is to introduce readers to key theological assumptions, decisions, themes, and commitments that drive Barth's theology. It is a guidebook offering resources for understanding Barth's theological vision and work as well as for assessing the pertinence of his theology to the reader's own context. It suggests a cluster of interpretive keys and signposts that will assist readers in recognizing the primary thematic and methodological movements in his work—in seeing what Barth is doing, having a sense of why he is doing it (in and for his own time and place), and assessing what it might mean *for us*, as readers of Barth early in the twenty-first century.[1] An early hint at a key theme: for Barth, Christian faith and its theology are always *directed*—directed by the free, living Word of God by which it is encountered, *if and when* it hears that Word—to address the concrete challenges and possibilities of the "here and now," of concrete contemporary contexts in all their distinctive particularity, complexity, and urgency.[2]

I attempt to be faithful to Barth's intentions, as I understand them, as he diagnoses what he believed to be the dangers, challenges, opportunities, and requirements of his own historical and theological context for faithful Christian witness to the gospel—again, as he understood it—and attempts

---

1. For a model of this approach, see Hunsinger, *How to Read Barth*. For another substantive introduction to Barth's theology, see Busch, *Great Passion*.

2. For Barth, revelation is always a concrete event that always occurs "here and now" (*sic et nunc*), which is always a new, living occurrence of what has occurred once for all, "there and then" (*illic et tunc*). See, for example, Barth, *Dogmatics* I/1, 148ff.; Barth, "Proclamation Here and Now."

to respond appropriately. The book also asks what those intentions, diagnoses, and the resulting concrete theological decisions and interventions might mean for us if we take Barth on as a theological conversation partner and resource, whether we read him generously, critically, or what is generally to be preferred, some relatively robust combination of both.

Ultimately, then, the primary audience for the book is the theologically interested pastor, layperson, and church congregation caught up in the daily struggles of life and of faith. It is for those attempting to discern the meaning of the gospel in and for the neighborhood, city, society, and world, and for their own lives as Christians living out their faith in those concrete contexts, in the struggles—sometimes mundane, sometimes historic—of discerning faithful and responsible (albeit always broken and sinful) Christian witness. Barth understood this witness to be focused on, bound to, and determined by (a) the unequivocal and uncompromisable goodness of the news about Jesus, and (b) the life of enacted belief which that news calls forth in creative Christian freedom and responsibility, communal and individual, to and for the broken world. Hint number two: for Barth, theology—even doctrinal/dogmatic theology—is never solely about nor completed with the sorting out of what the church believes, confesses, and proclaims in creeds and doctrinal standards and books of theology. It always also necessarily involves asking and answering the question: What then shall we *do*? How should we then *live*, here and now?[3]

The primary interest of the book, then, as introduction and companion to Barth's work, is in his theology's pertinence to the lives and faith of Christians and churches struggling to be living communities of witness in word and deed, in and for the neighborhood, society, and world. This means doing two things. First, it means assisting the reader in discovering and appreciating those dimensions in Barth's work that might yet function as life-affirming resources in resistance to destructive theological, ecclesial, and socio-political principalities and powers facing churches and societies today. Second, it means assisting the reader in recognizing and critically assessing all the ways in which Barth's theology is seen as both theologically

---

3. White evangelicals who were paying attention in the late 1970s will recognize this reference to Francis Schaeffer's book (and film series); see Schaeffer, *How Should We Then Live?* Barth's diagnosis of the maladies of twentieth-century Western culture, and prescription for what Christians and churches are called to do about it, are very different than Schaeffer's, while both purport to root their respective visions in the good news of the gospel. The subtitle of part 3 is taken from Schaeffer's book, an ironic highlighting of the divergence in their views of the gospel and what it might mean for concrete Christian ethical life.

and ethically problematic by both more conservative and more progressive theologians and persons of faith. This is particularly important in relation to all the destructive theological, ecclesial, and socio-political realities we are so painfully aware of in our own time that Barth—as a child of his times, despite his efforts to diagnose and critique those times in light of what he saw as the prophetic word of the gospel—did not see or feel the need to address, critique, and resist.

As important as it is to understand what Barth was doing and why in his own context, it is equally important to understand what so many contemporary readers of Barth find highly problematic in his theology, and why. Ultimately, of course, readers of this book and of Barth's own work have to come to their own assessment of how and to what extent Barth is friend or foe for churches and Christians today—and for everyone else!—and what he offers for their understanding of the life and work of faith in and for the world.

All cards on the table, then. The reader will find a generous reading of Barth in these pages. I am making a pitch, here. I want to propose that Barth's theology can function as a resource for Christians and churches today, particularly in all our conflictual diversity and polarization, and particularly in relation to the task of hearing and discerning anew (or, for many, what may feel like the first time) both the unequivocal goodness and universal embrace of the gospel news about Jesus, and the radically embodied life of concrete historical—social, political, economic—action and commitment that news calls the church into as a witnessing community in and for the world. (Another confession, then: I am more interested, both personally and with the writing of this book, in the ways in which Barth can be read as a theological resource for hearing the goodness of the news about Jesus—the news that God is unequivocally and irrevocably *for all*, but through the eye of a very specific and historically concrete needle: *the last, first!*—than in faithfulness to the letter of Barth's theology for its own sake.) At the same time, I hope to be clear about the ways in which this is a very hard sell for many, both on the theological left and the theological right of Barth. Barth—as with any theologian, historical or contemporary—can only function as a resource for churches and Christians today when generous readings proceed by way of *critical* engagement.

A GENERAL AUDIENCE, WITH AN EYE TO A PARTICULAR READER: THE PERPLEXED PROGRESSIVE/POST-EVANGELICAL

Beyond being a general introduction to Barth for a general audience, the book also has a more specific goal and a more specific audience. The more specific goal is to show how Barth provides resources for a particular theological and ethical possibility for today's Christians and churches that I believe is sorely needed in our ever more divisive and polemical climate, both in the churches and the nations. It is a possibility that is as widely overlooked as it is sorely needed: the possibility of a life of faith that is theologically traditional (relatively) and socio-politically progressive (in an *ad hoc* kind of way).

This brings us to the more specific audience that may find this introduction to Barth most interesting and most pertinent to the challenges of their particular context. I use the terms progressive evangelical or post-evangelical loosely and provisionally, without wanting to be limited by them, to locate the general ballpark of a certain kind of Christian experience. These terms are useful in this context for two reasons. First, they refer to what is likely to be a recognizable phenomenon for most Christians today, regardless of theological identity, and so function as a quick and efficient way to gesture toward the particular kind of Christian folk I have in mind. Second, having been raised and formed in and by a conservative evangelical community, I have found Barth to be a guide to my own perplexity with regard to the possibilities of wider, more inclusive, and more socio-politically progressive visions of the gospel news about Jesus. This personal experience determines my understanding and approach to Barth in ways that are likely to make this introduction to his work particularly pertinent to others shaped and marked in some way by what is generally referred to today as evangelicalism.

Beyond the limitations of these particular terms, the specific audience that I have in mind are Christian individuals, communities, and churches of any stripe who are relatively traditional theologically, i.e., in their confession of faith about Jesus and the gospel, yet find the conservative socio-political visions and commitments traditionally attached to and funded by that confession—for example, within the conservative white evangelicalism in the United States that has allowed itself to be co-opted as the most reliable demographic base of the Republican party and of what has become known as Trumpism—increasingly difficult to stomach. They find themselves increasingly attracted by more progressive socio-political visions of what the good news about Jesus means for creaturely life together on this planet, increasingly hungry for a gospel that, for example—recognizing what James Cone and others have helped us see as the unmistakable resonance between the cross and the lynching tree—is compelled by the urgency and necessity of the Black Lives Matter movement and prophetically critical of the idolatry of the Make America Great Again movement.[4]

However—and this is the perplexing part—the *theological* alternatives most commonly identified with those progressive socio-political visions are themselves progressive, involving what appear to be relatively radical and comprehensive reconstruction and sometimes rejection of central themes and commitments of traditional Christian faith. This leads to the commonly held assumption and expectation, on both sides of the theological spectrum, that one must become *theologically* progressive in order to be *socio-politically* progressive, that is, in order to have any theological grounds for committing to and living out progressive socio-political visions of the gospel as Christians and as churches.

This assumption and expectation results in two forms of perplexity for these increasingly progressively-minded people of traditional, confessional Christian faith. (a) For those who are not ready to give up the concrete content of their traditional confession of faith about God's redemption of the sinful world in Jesus (through the Spirit), it can seem as though the socio-political visions they find themselves increasingly compelled by and drawn to remain out of reach. (b) For others, also feeling the only option is to choose between traditional faith and progressive socio-political commitments, they reach a tipping point where the latter becomes too compelling to resist, and they let go of traditional Christian confession when—if they were aware of a viable alternative, such as is made visible by Barth's theology—they may not necessarily choose to do so. At the heart of this double-edged perplexity is the assumption that the *theological* spectrum of conservative-to-progressive is *necessarily* the same as the *socio-political* spectrum. Of course, it has often played out—and still does play out—this way historically, unfortunately. But it does not *have* to be this way. The theological and the socio-political are always essentially related and mutually implicating, but not always in the ways our habits of thinking and acting have led us to assume and expect.[5]

---

4. See Cone, *Cross and Lynching Tree*.

5. Dorothy Day and Walker Percy are examples of modern figures in the Roman Catholic tradition who attempted to inhabit this underpopulated territory of faith, in differing ways. However, Percy, like Barth, was not able to carry the theologically traditional/socio-politically progressive commitment consistently through to its implications for gender and sexuality, and was always more of a Southern moderate than a true progressive on race. Both Percy and Day remained on the conservative side of the abortion issue, as well. See Elie, *Life You Save*.

Consequently, this book offers an introduction and guide to Barth's theology that also addresses this perplexing blind spot. In doing so, it provides theologically traditional Christians the possibility of seeing how progressive socio-political visions and commitments can be rooted in (relatively) traditional confessions of the gospel news about God's redeeming action in and for the world in Jesus, through the Spirit.

Of course, Barth's is not the only theology that offers and enacts this possibility. This is a possibility that neither originates with nor is exclusive to Barth's theological vision and work. In the modern Anglo-European traditions, there are the Blumhardts (from whom Barth learned much), early Christian socialists (also an influence on Barth), the Mennonites, certain dimensions of Roman Catholic social teaching and its radical practitioners, such as Dorothy Day and Peter Maurin; included in the Roman Catholic tradition are liberation theologians from the southern hemisphere, most notably from Latin America, who see revolutionary political and economic commitments to be consistent with the teachings of the church and Scripture; in the various Black church traditions, producing civil rights leaders and activists, from Sojourner Truth to Martin Luther King Jr., there has always been a strong social dimension to the gospel, unlike most white evangelical traditions, particularly in relation to racism and poverty.[6]

Additionally, it must be said that Barth's work is wholly inadequate to this task when read on its own, especially in the hands of white, straight, economically privileged, cis-gendered males like me. Barth's work must not simply be supplemented by the voices of liberation, feminist, womanist, queer, disability, and eco theologies, but challenged, corrected, instructed, and often resisted by those voices and the experience and theological wisdom of the communities from which they emerge. This is absolutely necessary for Barth's best insights to be opened up to and function as a resource for the full depth and breadth of the socio-political goodness of the news about Jesus that Barth himself catches glimpses of within his own historical context. So, for the perplexed progressive evangelicals or post-evangelicals out there, together with any and all theologically traditional Christians thirsting for a vision of the radical social, political, and economic dimensions of the gospel news about Jesus, if you have not yet engaged liberation theologies, put down this book and read James Cone, Delores Williams, Gustavo Gutierrez,

---

6. Regarding the Blumhardts's influence on Barth, see Winn, *"Jesus Is Victor!"* I refer to Black churches and Black church traditions in the plural in light of conversations with my colleague, the Rev. Dr. Gary Simpson. He believes the traditional reference to *the* Black church erases important multiplicities and differences among Black churches and Black folks of Christian faith.

Rosemary Radford Reuther, Audre Lorde, Carter Heyward, and Nancy Eiesland—and this is just for starters; these are all publically recognized pillars of mid- to late-twentieth-century liberationist revolutions in theology, leaving both much researching and much catching up to do. Then pick this book back up along with whatever work by Barth you have on the shelf or got for Christmas and we can get to work.

PART 1

APPROACHING BARTH'S THEOLOGY

What Is Theology about and What Is at Stake?

1

I'VE GOT ONE WORD
FOR YOU: JESUS CHRIST

When approaching Barth's theology, I believe our chances of understanding what he is doing and why are increased if we keep two things in mind: Barth is really ever only trying to say one thing, and that one thing is wholly, unadulterated good news for the creature and for creation. Keeping these two insights in front of us as the primary lenses through which we read his work will help us keep our eyes on the ball of his fundamental concerns and intentions. In this way, whether we agree or disagree with Barth, we will at least have some assurance that we are within the ballpark of reading him well.

This chapter focuses on the first theme, that Barth is really ever only trying to say one thing. The following chapter will focus on the second theme, his conviction that this one thing is wholly and unequivocally good news.

IT'S JUST THAT SIMPLE—WELL, ALMOST: THE ONE DIVINE WORD AND THE INEXHAUSTIBILITY OF CREATURELY WITNESS

Barth has written so many pages, and there has been so much written about those pages by others, determining where to begin and what to say in the few pages available to us here can be a daunting task. Happily, Barth himself is quite accommodating in this regard. In fact, it often seems that Barth himself is saying the same thing over and over again in different ways, in different contexts. Indeed, I believe this is precisely what he is trying to do, what he sees himself as doing—what he sees as the task of all church speaking and action, including its work of theology.

This, then, would seem a good place to start in one's attempt to come to grips with the vast corpus of Barth's theology. It is our first interpretive key to unlocking what lies at the heart of all those pages. I propose that, on every page, in every book, in every presentation, in every sermon—*if and when* he is being consistent with and faithful to his own fundamental insights, convictions, and commitments—Barth is ever only trying to hear, think through, and repeat what he believes to be the one eternal, divine Word that has been spoken and enacted to and for the world, the one Word that constitutes the entirety of the church's faith, life, and task as a community called to witness to that Word with its own words and actions. He is trying to listen for this Word, point to it the best he can, and discern what that one Word means for us in every concrete context: what it says to us, what it promises us, what it assures us of, what it warns us about, what it judges us for, what it *does to* and *for* us, what it liberates us from, what it calls us to do.

That one Word—okay, two words, or more accurately, a name and a title—is Jesus Christ. Barth believed that this one name, a first name and a title—*when truly heard and acknowledged*—includes all that the church has to hear, and then to say and to live out to and for the world. This and nothing more; but definitely *this* (as Barth would say). The critical question for us, then: What exactly does Barth believe is included in this one name and title, Jesus Christ, when truly heard and acknowledged? What does the church say when it says "Jesus Christ"?

For Barth, when the church says the name (and title) Jesus Christ, it is only pointing to and attempting to repeat what it believes to be the one eternal Word that *God* has spoken, not only about, to, and for the creature and creation, but primarily about, to, and for *Godself*. For Barth, Jesus Christ is the one Word of God in the sense that, in the personal reality, history, and event that is God with and for us in Jesus of Nazareth (through the power of the Holy Spirit)—in the context of God's journey with Israel among and for the nations—God has eternally willed, decided, and made concretely actual who God is and who we are and what creation is, once for all. More particularly, God has eternally willed and decided, once for all, to be only and wholly, unequivocally, irrevocably, irreversibly with and for—indeed, *as*—the creature in the concrete, person, history, event, and relation that both *occurs in* and *is* Jesus Christ (in the Spirit); and that, in that same person, history, event, and relation, the creature is and will be for God, and in God, for one another and for the goodness of all creation. More particularly, still: in Jesus

Christ (through the Spirit), God is for us, sinners, and not against us—for us *all*, each and every one, *the last, first*—and we are for God, and in God, for each other, *the last, first. Period.*[1]

What is theology about, then, for Barth? For Barth, there is no other divine will, decision, Word, or act concerning Godself, the creature, or creation. All of God's thoughts about, desires for, and dealings with creation and the creature are decided and determined in this one, eternal, divine will, decision, Word, and act, as is the meaning and future of all creaturely life and activity. Consequently, for Barth—and this is key—that to which the church points when it confesses Jesus Christ comprehends, encloses, and determines all of history—both God's and creation's. That which occurs and is decided and made actual in Jesus Christ (through the Spirit) is nothing less than the whole Trinitarian sweep of God's dealing with creation from before the foundations of the world to the fulfillment of history in the fulfilled and unbroken communion of God with creature and creature with and in God.[2] When the church confesses Jesus Christ, then, it undertakes its commission to say this one thing and only this one thing: God is wholly, unqualifiedly, and irreversibly with and for the creature and creation in Jesus (through the power of the Spirit). And in saying this it communicates the essential content of the entire Trinitarian drama from before creation through to its fulfillment in the eschaton.[3]

When encountering Barth's repeated references to Jesus Christ as the one Word of God, it is all too easy to fall into traditional default views that see only the Second Person of the Trinity incarnate in Jesus of Nazareth as

---

1. The way in which Barth understands both who *God* is and who *we* are to be determined in Jesus Christ is most explicitly laid out in his doctrine of election. See Barth, *Dogmatics* II/2; see especially, "Jesus Christ, Electing and Elected," 94–145.

2. See, for example: As the Word of God, Jesus Christ is "God's decree and God's beginning. He is so all-inclusively, comprehending absolutely within Himself all things and everything, enclosing within Himself the autonomy of all other words, decrees, and beginnings" (Barth, *Dogmatics* II/2, 95).

3. Barth makes it clear in the first volume of his *Church Dogmatics* that the Word of God that occurs and takes place in and as Jesus Christ is the content of the divine Trinitarian life and work. See parts I, II, and III of vol. I (the last two hundred pages of vol. I, pt. 1, and all of vol. I, pt. 2). His doctrine of the Word of God turns out to be nothing other than his doctrine of the Trinity. See also: "Revelation in fact does not differ from the person of Jesus Christ nor from the reconciliation accomplished in Him . . . When in the word revelation we say 'The Word was made flesh and dwelt among us,' then we are saying something which can have only an intertrinitarian basis in the will of the Father and the sending of the Son and the Holy Spirit, in the eternal decree of the triune God, so that it can be established only as knowledge of God from God" (Barth, *Dogmatics* I/1, 119). See also Barth, "Revelation," 13–19.

God's means of providing the human being a remedy for sin and so a way of staying out of hell. If and when we do, we lose sight of the entire Trinitarian eternal-historical drama that is entailed in and signified by Barth's deployment of the name, Jesus Christ; a drama that begins with God's relationship *to Godself* before the foundations of the world. Consequently, simply repeating the frequency of Barth's own references to that name does not itself ensure that we are hearing and seeing what Barth is intending. As we will see more clearly as we go, for Barth, the name Jesus Christ always refers to the living, Trinitarian history between God and the creature within creation, in the midst of which we find ourselves addressed and called into responsible, active participation.[4] The content of the name Jesus Christ as the one Word of God is always a narrative, both enacted once for all and eternally open. Consequently, when thinking theologically with Barth, it is of vital importance that we are continually reminded of what the church is—or is supposed to be—pointing to when it says the name Jesus Christ: not only an *individual person*, albeit a divine-human one, but a living *history* of divine—and human (as we will see)—*decision, action, event,* and *personal relation*, the epic sweep of which embraces all creatures, all of history and all of creation. For Barth, to say the name Jesus Christ as the one Word of God properly one has to tell the (ongoing, unfolding) story of the gospel as unqualified and all-embracing good news.[5]

What, then, for Barth, is at stake in theology? As we will see, for Barth, the primary importance of there being only this one divine Word and no other—God with and for us all in Jesus (through the Spirit), the last, first—is that no room is left for another word or any number of other words: for

---

4. See, for example: "In Jesus Christ there is no isolation of man from God or of God from man. Rather, in Him we encounter the history, the dialogue, in which God and man meet together and are together, the reality of the covenant *mutually* contracted, preserved, and fulfilled by them" (Barth, "Humanity of God," 46).

5. For Barth's judgment of the comparatively limited scope of the conservative evangelical vision of what occurs in Jesus Christ, see, for example: "Can one read . . . even as much as two chapters from the Bible and still with good conscience say, God's word went forth to humanity, his mandate guided history from Abraham to Christ, the Holy Spirit descended in tongues of fire upon the apostles at Pentecost, a Saul became a Paul and traveled over land and sea—all in order that here and there specimens of men like you and me might be 'converted' . . . and by a redeeming death go some day to 'heaven.' Is *that* all? . . . The powerful forces which come to expression in the Bible, the movements of peoples, the battles, and the convulsions which take place before us there, the miracles and revelations which constantly occur there, the immeasurable promises for the future which are unceasingly repeated to us there—do not all these things stand in a rather strange relation to so small a result—if that is really the only result they have?" (Barth, "Strange New World," 46).

example, that God is or might be against us; or is simply indifferent; or is for some of us but not others; or is not for the last, first, but is for the powerful and privileged, first; or is for us but only on certain conditions, as reward for purity or fealty; or only on certain days or seasons or according to divine whims; or that we are not to be wholly and unequivocally for each other and for all of creation; or that we are to be only for some others but not all; or that in being for all we are not necessarily to be for the last, first, but for the powerful and privileged, first. For Barth, the church has only one thing to say because God has only willed, decided, said, and done one thing in relation to both God and creature: God for us all, the last, first, and us for God, and in God, for each other, the last, first. And Barth understands this one thing to be a wholly good thing, a wholly good Word.

In beginning to understand what Barth means by Jesus Christ (in the Spirit) as the content of God's eternal will, decision, Word, and action, and the history of relation between God and creature enacted therein, as well as of the church's confession, proclamation, and embodied witness in the creativity and responsibility of Christian freedom, we are well on our way to understanding what Barth is trying to get at with every word on every page, at least with regard to his best intentions. For Barth, every word, every affirmation, every critique, every dispute, every biblical exegesis, every doctrine, every methodological decision is only important in relation to the publishing and living out of this news. And Barth is open to finding *ad hoc* allies in any human words or actions—either inside or outside the church; either religious, spiritual, or secular—that help point to and live out this news and its goodness. Correspondingly, he will argue with any human word or action—both inside and outside the church—that he believes diminishes the radical extent to which God is for us all, for each and every one, the last, first, or suggests that God is or even might be against us or against our neighbor or against even those who desire to be our enemy; that is, any word that diminishes what he believes to be the radical goodness of the gospel news.

This notion of the *one thing*, then, will be a signpost by which we will orient, guide, and limit our approach to Barth's vast corpus. We will be looking for the fundamental themes in Barth's understanding of this one thing, for how it determines the *way* in which Christians and churches are to think, speak, and act theologically, and for *what* it constrains Christians and churches to say and do in their spoken and embodied witness in, to, and for the world

THEN WHY SO MANY WORDS OVER SO MANY PAGES?

This issue of the *one thing*—of there being only one eternal, divine Word the church is commissioned to hear and to repeat—may all seem fairly straightforward thus far. However, if you have some familiarity with Barth's work, you are no doubt asking yourself: If it is that simple, if that is all that needs to be said, then why does Barth seem almost comically incapable of coming to the end of theology? (Having published the first part-volume of the *Church Dogmatics* in 1932, Barth still had at least one more [no doubt multi-part] volume of the already massive project to go when he died in 1968.) We've already caught a glimpse of one reason why, after a gazillion pages, Barth was still not finished writing about what the church confesses to itself and to the world when it says Jesus Christ (in the Spirit): to say Jesus Christ (in the Spirit) is to speak of the entire Trinitarian journey, both within Godself and with creation, from before the foundations of the world to the consummation of history in the eschaton. That is quite a bit to unpack.

There are, however, several other reasons why, for Barth, it takes a lifetime to say what needs to be said when confessing the name Jesus Christ (in the Spirit) as the *one* divine Word to and for the creature and all creation. I will just briefly raise them here. We will revisit these issues more in depth in the following chapters.

First, the one Word that is God for us in Jesus (through the Spirit) is a fundamentally paradoxical business. Theology can only say this one thing by saying two very different, even seemingly contradictory things, at the same time. For example: on one hand, Jesus is fully human, and on the other hand, Jesus is fully God; on one hand, God is God and we are sinful creatures and never the twain shall meet, yet on the other hand, God and sinners do in fact meet, yea, are united, in the most intimate relation of fellowship and communion; on one hand, we have no natural capacity to know God and so do not and cannot know God, but on the other hand, we really do know God in God's free, miraculous self-giving; on one hand, God is never at our disposal, to be grasped by creaturely control, while on the other hand, God genuinely gives Godself to us to be known and loved and, yes, held.

To say this one thing, then—or more accurately, to say everything that is entailed in this one thing: that God is for us wholly and irrevocably in Jesus (through the Spirit)—theology must think and speak dialectically. It must move back and forth between (at least) two affirmations that, in and of themselves, seem to be in contradiction to one another and yet must both be confirmed as true. It must say one thing in the strongest possible terms, then say the apparently opposite thing just as strongly, without taking back the first thing; it must make very clear that, how, and why something is impossible for the creature, then assert in no uncertain terms that not only is it possible, it is *actual*—as a *divine* possibility—without rescinding the assertion of its creaturely impossibility. And there is no end to this dialectical back and forth for creaturely witness to this paradoxical reality and history. In order to say the *one thing* that needs to be said, there is always more than one thing that needs to be said; but going on to affirm the dialectical counterpart of whatever is said cannot itself be the final word, for it does not replace the first thing said, but is to be held in dialectical tension with it. So the first affirmation must then be reiterated so as not to be lost from view—and so it goes. The need to speak dialectically is the need to *keep* speaking.[6] If Christian theology does not think and speak in this dialectical way, then it cannot say the one thing—the *only* thing—it *must* say: God is *for* us, sinners all. At least, it cannot say it faithfully and obediently. At least, not according to Barth.

Reading tip: This back and forth of dialectical movement—on one hand . . . ; but on the other hand . . . ; but don't forget the *first* hand . . . ; and on and on—constitutes the rhythm of much if not all of Barth's writing. This is an opportune spot, then, to offer a tip for reading Barth along these lines. The tip: *keep reading*. If you come across something you don't like in Barth, keep reading, he is likely to qualify and counter it with the other side of the dialectical movement required by the subject matter that is God for us sinners in Jesus (through the Spirit). You may not like the counter point that is coming either, but in light of it, you will understand the initial point better. Similarly, if you come across something you like in Barth, keep reading. Chances are he is about to complicate it in a way that you may not like or that will at least modify your understanding of the initial point. To keep reading does not guarantee you will eventually like Barth more or even at all. It only increases your chances of understanding him better, and of being better able to make an informed and responsible assessment.

Second, the one, eternal, divine Word that takes place in God's decision and act to be for us in Jesus (through the Spirit) can require many creaturely words in the church's attempt to bear witness to it because the reality of that

---

6. However, as we will see, this is not the same as infinite progression of equally balanced yet contradictory terms. This is especially true and important for Barth in relation to the divine Yes and No of salvation and judgment. On one hand, *for our work of theology*, both must always be said, and we must always go back and forth, because neither word can ever be the last and so only word on its own. However, we must do this in a way that makes clear that the No is always bracketed by the Yes, and so, *in God*—and in that way, *for us*—the Yes, while always entailing a No, is nevertheless the first and last word of God to the creature: "No Yes and No but only Yes." See, for example, Barth, *Dogmatics* I/1, 226–27. See also Barth, "Sovereignty of God's Word," 31–32.

Word occurs as a *history* of personal encounter and relation. For Barth, the one Word to which the church's confession of Jesus Christ (in the Spirit) points is a *living* Word. As such, it constitutes a history of living personal *encounter*, a living history of divine call and creaturely response, a continual speaking and acting in and for the world. It is a Word of living encounter and relation that is addressed to the creature, again and again, to be heard and believed and responded to with one's life, ever anew, ever again, till the end of time.[7]

We are caught up in this living history of personal address and encounter, of divine call and creaturely response. In the midst of this history, we are interrupted and addressed by a divine Word and act that is not our own, which we can neither anticipate nor control, and to which we find ourselves called to respond. We are unable to step outside of this history of event and encounter and view it from some objective vantage point or fixed, stationary, universal horizon, at rest and at our leisure in the repose of reflection, from which vantage point we can take its measure, mark its beginning and end, and comprehend it completely in creaturely word and concept as a rounded off whole. On the contrary, the one Word of God, for Barth, is something that *happens to us*, interrupts us, claims us, and calls for a response, calling us into action—into creaturely word and act that is always only response *in medias res*. Because the one Word that is God for us in Jesus (through the Spirit) is a *living* Word of personal address and encounter, it calls ever anew for living words and acts of creaturely response and witness. The one divine Word calls forth creaturely words and acts of witness without end.

Third, and finally, for now, there is no end to what must be said or written or done when one says or writes or lives one's witness to what God wills and makes actual in Jesus Christ (through the Spirit) because there are so many ways to get it wrong. And Christians and churches have consistently insisted on getting it wrong in every possible way in every possible context throughout Christianity's long and troubling histories, with very little sign of ever letting up. Indeed, for Barth, the histories of the churches could be read as the histories of continually getting the one thing Christians and churches need to say and do wrong, while working tirelessly—or lazily or indifferently, depending on the context—to say and do many and various other things,

---

7. See, for example: What God's Word is "is something God . . . must constantly tell us afresh" (Barth, *Dogmatics* I/1, 132); "To stand in faith means to be called to new faith . . . being directed anew to the free actualization of the grace experience, clinging anew to the promise, looking anew for the event in which the possibility of knowledge of God's Word comes into view for us . . . When we know it, we *expect* to know it" (Barth, *Dogmatics* I/1, 225; my emphasis).

sometimes interesting and even good things, but just as often bad and terribly destructive things, and ultimately, at the end of the day, anything other than the one thing they are called and commissioned to say and do.

Again, for Barth, churches and Christians, together with their creeds, doctrines, preaching, and, yes, even their Scriptures, always remain fully and thoroughly human and so not only finite, but sinful, with all the frailty and risk and inevitability of serious damage that this entails (more on Barth's distinctive qualifications with regard to Scripture in the next chapter). This requires continual vigilance. We can never stop the work of confession and repentance, which includes the theological work of self-interrogation, self-critique, and self-correction, as part of a new hearing, speaking, and doing.

Yes, for Barth, the church always only has one Word to hear and to repeat in word and deed as best it can. But because of what this one Word *is* and *does*, the church's hearing and repeating of this Word, and the creaturely words and actions it employs in attempting to faithfully repeat this Word, can never be exhausted, can never come to an end, can never arrive at a final human, creaturely word or deed. For Barth, the church can never stop hearing, writing, speaking, living, and enacting anew what it believes to be the one living Word of God for us, each and every one, sinners all, the last, first, in Jesus (through the Spirit). It can never stop confessing and proclaiming that one Word, with all the various words and deeds—both big and small, fancy and plain, sophisticated and simple, theoretical and practical, political and personal—that confessing and proclaiming that one Word in Christian freedom and responsibility may entail in any given context.

This idea that Barth really only attempts to say one thing, or to serve the saying of this one thing by Christians and churches, on every page he has written, is our first signpost for orienting ourselves in relation to his work, our first interpretive key for understanding what Barth is trying to say and do, and why. If you are looking for how Barth is attempting to say, to repeat, to exegete, to explicate, to witness to what he believes to be the one eternal, divine Word that is *God for us all in Jesus Christ (through the Spirit), the last, first, and us for God, and in God, for each other, the last first* (he is unfortunately not as consistent with "the last, first" as he is with the "all"), on whatever page of whatever book by Barth you happen to pick up, you are orienting yourself in a fruitful way; you are starting in the right place—no matter where you start—and looking in the right direction. Consequently, you are increasing your chances of hearing what Barth is trying to say, and why, whether you like what he is trying to say, and why he is trying to say it, or not.

THREE MATTERS OF STYLE

Finally, I will be employing three stylistic conventions to (a) signal two consistent critiques of Barth's particular form of Christocentrism—i.e., Jesus Christ as the *one* divine Word that needs to be said, heard, and lived—and to (b) function, in a minor way, as corrective. First, I will often refer to the name Jesus where Barth almost invariably uses the name/title Jesus Christ. This is to signal what I believe to be Barth's lack of consistent attention to the full humanity of Jesus in its detail and richness, particularly its social, economic, and political dimensions. In reading Barth, it is easy to lose sight of Jesus of Nazareth in the bright light of his focus on the fact that it is *God* who is fully and wholly with and for us in this Jesus.[8] This can have the effect of hiding from view the full socio-historical dimensions of the salvation that is accomplished in Jesus (through the Spirit), and that Barth himself, I believe, would not necessarily want to deny or obscure. That Jesus is the Christ, for Barth—God truly with us in the flesh, uniquely, fully, and salvifically—should be assumed by the reader. My stylistic convention merely intends to keep the full dimensions of the creaturely humanity of Jesus Christ before us, to counter the way in which the divinity implied in the title of Christ can tend to eclipse that humanity in Barth's usage.

Second and relatedly, I consistently include the phrase, *the last, first*, in my shorthand formula for what Barth believes to occur in Jesus Christ. This is another way of highlighting the *concreteness* of what God says and does in the particular history and person of Jesus Christ that Barth is so insistent upon and determined that we not lose sight of. This concreteness includes the historical, social, cultural, political, and economic dimensions of the actual flesh in and with which God chooses to fully disclose and give Godself to the creature, what James Cone refers to as the social location of Jesus of Nazareth—God shows up in a lowly manger, on the margins of a community that is itself oppressed by European empire, not in the palace of that very empire; and what is more, God in Jesus is legally executed by that empire as a threat to law and order, i.e., to its sovereignty and control. If God gives Godself fully to and for the creature and creation in *this* Jesus (through the Spirit), then the socio-historical dimensions of the concrete life of this Jesus are not accidental. They reveal both the heart of who God is in Godself and the concrete *way* in which God is salvifically with and for all: *the last, first*. And, of course, this particular concreteness of God's *way* of salvific engagement with and for creation is given witness in the biblical testimony to Jesus,

---

8. See Cone, *God of the Oppressed*, 107.

including the reported words and deeds of Jesus himself, in his own ministry and teaching. Alas, Barth often appears to overlook this particular dimension of the very concreteness of God's decision, Word, and act in Jesus Christ that he is otherwise so insistent upon. My stylistic convention attempts to be faithful to Barth's insistence upon concreteness where Barth himself can be read as failing to do so. The implications of this insistence are most explicitly addressed in chapters 6 and 7.

Third, as the reader has no doubt noticed by now, I parenthetically attach the Spirit to each mention of Jesus or Jesus Christ. This is intended to signal the way in which Barth's use of the name Jesus Christ as a shorthand for the whole Trinitarian, eternal-historical drama he is always meaning to signify can function to erase the distinctive Person and work of the Holy Spirit in this Trinitarian drama. This unintentional effect is enabled by the long history of traditional theological habits of thinking, especially in the West, which focus on "Father" and "Son" in the Trinitarian relations and drama of salvation, and for which the Spirit is consistently a latecomer, if not an afterthought, to the Trinitarian party. For Barth, Jesus Christ does not only mean the divine decision, Word, act, and event in which God is concretely with and for us, from eternity to eternity; that name also always means a Trinitarian history that occurs only in and through the power of the Holy Spirit.[9]

QUESTIONS

1. What is Christian theology supposed to be about, for Barth? What does he think is at stake? That is, what does he think is threatened if we get it "wrong"? What is to be gained if we get it "right"? What do *you* think might be risked in and by *Barth's* understanding of and approach to theology?

2. Why does Barth write so many words if he is ever only trying to say one thing, i.e., "Jesus Christ"?

3. What does it mean to think of Jesus Christ as Trinitarian event, act, history, and relation? That is, according to Barth, what are the different things the church says when it says, "Jesus Christ"? Put differently, what occurs, for Barth, in the divine Word and act that is God for us in Jesus Christ (through the Spirit)?

---

9. Barth did not live to finish his final volume of *Church Dogmatics*, which would have been his fully fleshed-out doctrine of the Holy Spirit, but for a helpful, concise glimpse of his thinking on the Spirit, see Barth, *Holy Spirit and Christian Life*.

4. How does Barth's view of what occurs in Jesus Christ differ from your view (if it does, in fact, differ)? How is that difference a challenge to think, speak, believe, act differently? Do you view that challenge as a dangerous threat or a resourceful invitation? Why? In what ways?

5. What would it mean to read every biblical passage and understand every Christian doctrine through the lens of Barth's view of Jesus Christ as the one Word of God to and for all creatures and creation? Give examples in relation to specific biblical texts and/or Christian doctrines.

2

THE NEWS IS GOOD
God Is for Us, Period

THE GOODNESS OF THE NEWS

FOR BARTH, THE CHURCH has only one thing to say because God has only willed, decided, said, and done one thing in relation to both God and creature. And this one thing is a wholly good thing, a wholly good Word: God is only and wholly for us all, the last, first, and we are for God, and in God, for each other, the last, first. Another key signpost, then, for understanding at least the intention of Barth's work—perhaps the most important of our signposts—is the depth, breadth, and consistency of his conviction that the gospel news about Jesus is truly, only, and wholly good. It is "unalloyed" good news.[1] It is, in fact, for Barth, the best possible news that the human creature—and creation itself—could ever possibly hear.[2] It is certainly not a mixture of good news and bad news. It is not a "mixed message of joy and terror," as Barth puts

---

1. Cunningham, "Barth's Interpretation of Ephesians," 1.

2. See, for example: "The doctrine of election is the sum of the gospel because of all words that can be said or heard it is the best: that God elects man; that God is for man too the One who loves in freedom" (Barth, *Dogmatics* II/2, 3); "it is the best news, the wholly redemptive news . . . This movement [of God towards the creature] is always the very best thing that could happen to man. The reality and revelation of this movement is Jesus Christ himself" (*Dogmatics* II/2, 91–92).

it: good news for some (Christians, believers, the elect, the saved), but very bad news for everyone else.[3]

Barth believes this to be the case for everything the churches hear and know and have to say in the one Word that is God for us in Jesus (through the Spirit). For Barth, the gospel—i.e., this good news about Jesus—does not refer only to the parts of the biblical witness or of doctrines or of creedal confessions that deal with salvation, distinct from sin and judgment. For Barth, the news that is wholly good is the news of both the judgment of sin and the salvation of the sinner; of both the wrath of God and the love and mercy of God. This is likely to sound very strange for most folks familiar with the church's traditional ways of treating the themes of salvation and judgment.

Perhaps the clearest expression of Barth's distinctive conviction on this point is his doctrine of election. Barth opens his doctrine of election by calling election the best word any creature could ever possibly hear. Now, this is the *Reformed* doctrine of election we're talking about (well, at least *a version* of it), complete with double predestination!—the one doctrine most reviled by all Christians and churches, except, perhaps, for the most hardcore TULIP Calvinists, as the most horrific thing the church has ever cooked up.[4] Yes, *this* doctrine of election, with all its divine wrath, rejection, reprobation, and judgment, this is what Barth calls the best possible word ever addressed to the creature. That is a mind-boggling claim. And either Barth is crazy or a sadist (possibilities we shouldn't discount out of hand, of course), *or* he is seeing and hearing something that the theological lenses most of us are familiar with do not see or hear; something that is radically counterintuitive and that turns the theological habits of thinking of both conservative and progressive theological traditions on their head.

What Barth sees and hears in the doctrine of election is, of course, Jesus Christ (in the Spirit). Put differently, what he sees and hears is a doctrine of election, complete with (albeit his own version of) double predestination, that can only mean what it means for both church and world when its content—both election and rejection, salvation and reprobation, mercy and judgment—is wholly and strictly determined by what is known in Jesus Christ, by what God has decided, willed, and enacted regarding Godself and creation in that one Word, reality, history, person, event, and relation that is God for

---

3. Barth, *Dogmatics* II/2, 13.

4. TULIP is an acronym for what has long since been the five pillars of a certain strand of Calvinist orthodoxy: total depravity; unconditional election; limited atonement; irresistible grace; perseverance of the saints. Limited atonement is the real killer: God does not, in fact, will that all be saved, so the saving, atoning blood of Jesus is intended and efficacious only for the elect, not for all. Ouch!

us *all*, sinners, in Jesus (through the Spirit), the last, first. We will have more to say about this later. Here we can simply say that whatever divine rejection, reprobation, judgment, and wrath is included in the biblical witness to, and the doctrinal inheritance of, election and predestination, those themes can only signify the extent to which they are fundamentally limited and ultimately overcome by God's eternal will, decision, and act to be *only* for us and not against us—precisely *as sinners*—in Jesus (through the Spirit).[5] It cannot signify anything other than God as unequivocally, irreversibly, irrevocably, unqualifiedly for us and not against us. Yes, there is rejection, reprobation, judgment, and wrath in God's unreserved no to the destructiveness of sin and death. But, as *from God,* and as its content is determined, grounded in, and limited by God's one eternal will, decision, Word, and action to be *only for* us in Jesus (through the Spirit), divine wrath and rejection et al. cannot mean the destruction of the creature, of any creature—period. Quite the contrary. It can only mean the salvation of the creature, our reconciliation to God in fellowship and communion, and in God, to and with one another. (It is here, in Barth's emphasis on the *all*, on the universal embrace of God's electing decision in Jesus Christ, that he appears to most often forget about *the last, first,* that is also entailed in the historical concreteness of that decision.)

This is a pivotal acid test for "getting" Barth. If you can see how and why he can say that the doctrine of election, albeit *his version* of it—complete with double predestination (which, as determined by God for us in Jesus, through the Spirit, is *not* Calvin's double predestination)[6]—is the sum of the gospel

---

5. See, for example, Barth, *Dogmatics* II/2, 94–145. See especially: "In Jesus Christ God in His free grace determines Himself for sinful man and sinful man for Himself . . . He [Jesus Christ] is the election of God before which and without which and beside which God cannot make any other choices. Before Him and without Him and beside Him God does not, then, elect or will anything . . . As the subject and object of this choice [God's eternal electing decision] Jesus Christ was at the beginning . . . He was at the beginning of all things, at the beginning of God's dealings with the reality which is distinct from Himself" (Barth, *Dogmatics* II/2, 94–103).

6. Calvin's doctrine of double predestination says that God's eternal decree—the *decretum absolutum*—determines two things concerning the human creature, expressing two divine wills and separating creatures into two categories with two eternal destinations: some are predestined to salvation and eternity with God (the elect); the rest are predestined to condemnation and eternal judgment (the reprobate). Barth's version says that God has only *one* eternal will and makes only *one* eternal decision: to be wholly for, and not against, the human creature. However, this one will and decision concerns two parties, God and the sinful creature, and so the "double" nature of predestination is preserved, but with a wholly different outcome: God chooses Godself to be only for the sinful creature, and chooses the sinful creature to be for God; God chooses the destructive consequences of sin for Godself, and chooses a future of reconciled fellowship with God for the sinful creature, etc.

and, as such, the best of all possible words any creature could hear, then you are getting at the heart of his theological vision and commitments. (More on this in chapters 4 and 5.)

BARTH'S "NEIN!" TO NATURAL THEOLOGY

One of the things Barth is infamous for is his unequivocal no—complete with exclamation point—to what he calls natural theology.[7] I say infamous because this is one of the shibboleth issues that divides opinion on Barth. You either love him or hate him because of this no. What Barth means by natural theology will become more and more clear as we go. For now, a quick technical definition. For Barth, natural theology includes any theology that attempts to ground itself methodologically upon anything that is available to human knowledge and experience of ourselves and the world in a natural, general way through either nature, reason, or history—including what we call religious history and experience—apart from the way God gives Godself to be known and loved in the particular, free, and contingent event of divine self-disclosure in Jesus (through the Spirit). Barth's own shorthand for natural theology: "Natural theology is the doctrine of a union of humanity with God existing outside God's revelation in Jesus Christ."[8] In short, Barth rejects as the ground for theology anything that can be said to be at our disposal and direction, within the realm of our spontaneity and our agency—even a presumably God-given agency—and so in some way under our control.

For Barth, the classic paradigm of natural theology is Thomas Aquinas's "analogy of being." Borrowing from Aristotle, Aquinas saw the human being, together with all creatures and creation, as an effect of the divine "first cause." As such, we are able to begin with our knowledge of ourselves and of creation—as creaturely effects of the divine cause—and use our God-given reason to walk our way up the down escalator of being, as it were, by and through which we receive our creaturely being from God. If we do so properly, we can—upon reaching the top of the down escalator, through the disciplined use of reason—attain to analogical but reliable truths about God.[9] However, for Barth, natural theology was not limited to Aquinas's analogy of being, or to the Roman Catholic tradition more generally. On the contrary,

---

7. Barth, "Nein!," 65–128. The preface and sections II and III of Barth's six-part essay, helpfully set in historical and theological context, can also be found in Green, *Theologian of Freedom*, 151–67.

8. Barth, *Dogmatics* II/1, 168.

9. See Aquinas, *Summa Theologica* I; see especially questions 12, 13, 14.

Barth understood natural theology to come in many different forms, shapes, and sizes.

I suggest the best way to approach what Barth means by natural theology and why he is so worried about it—that is, what he sees to be *at stake* in natural theology—is through his commitment to what he believes to be the unadulterated goodness of the gospel news. Barth's understanding of and polemic against natural theology is of a piece with his call for an incessant vigil keeping watch for all the ways in which Christians and churches turn the good news of the gospel into bad news by turning it into something that is under the interpretive control of some human possibility, some human word or system or program or method. For Barth, this can happen—and does happen; is always happening—in the ancient Roman Catholic tradition, in seventeenth- and eighteenth-century Protestant orthodoxies, in nineteenth-century liberal theologies and conservative pietisms, and in twentieth-century biblicist fundamentalisms. The list goes on. As Barth sees it, natural theology requires our most rigorous theological vigilance and resistance because it is *always occurring* on *all sides*. Indeed, from Barth's viewpoint, there are as many examples as there are theologies and theologians, denominations and churches. It is particular neither to one nor to a certain number of traditions or denominations, nor to one side of theological or socio-political spectrums. Rather, it is always ample and thriving in every corner and at every turn. And again, most importantly, for Barth, wherever and whenever it thrives it inevitably threatens to diminish the goodness of the news.

Here is the tricky bit. As we have seen, Barth is always trying to demonstrate how the content of who God is and what God has done in Jesus (through the Spirit) is only and wholly good, is cause for only thanksgiving and joy. However, what Barth understands to be the source, ground, and guarantee of the goodness of the news about Jesus—that it is first and last *from God*, willed and enacted in radical divine freedom, and so never under our control as a human religious project, to preserve, to keep safe, to defend, to certify, to ensconce, to enshrine—this is precisely what Christians and churches throughout history have shown we fear most, as the *worst* possible news: that *we* are not in control; that God's decisive and determining Word and action is not at our disposal, not submitted for our approval, certification, and verification, nor subject to our policing power.[10]

---

10. See, for example: "The goal of all yearning in theology is to be able to do this [i.e., to say what the Word of God is], but this is the goal of an illegitimate yearning" (Barth, *Dogmatics* I/1, 164).

That is to say, *from the point of view of natural theology,* it is *Barth* who poses the threat to the goodness of the gospel. Indeed, what Barth calls natural theology is always ample and thriving on all sides and in all traditions of the entire church because it understands itself to be protecting, preserving, retrieving, and/or liberating the true goodness of what the church has traditionally called the gospel news about Jesus. This is true for both the left and the right, for the progressive as for the conservative; as true for the liberal Protestant as for the Roman Catholic as for the conservative evangelical.[11]

However, *from Barth's point of view,* it is what he sees as natural theology's anxious attempt to domesticate divine freedom—to bring God and God's Word and action within the presumed protective parameters of theology's governing wisdom, to place God under the safety of its system of checks and balances—that always threatens to and inevitably does diminish the goodness of the news about Jesus (in the Spirit).

Another signpost, then: For Barth, the greatest and most consistent danger to the goodness of the gospel is the human desire for mastery and control of that very goodness, and so of God, self, and neighbor—*even when it is for the sake of protecting and guaranteeing that goodness!* Every critical and polemical move that Barth makes, then—or at least the *intention* behind these moves—can be seen as in some way related to his effort to identify, critique, and resist all the myriad ways and means and guises and disguises of this desire for possession of and mastery over what he understands to be the Word of God and so over God Godself, which always involves a destructive mastery over the neighbor.[12]

---

11. This constitutes much of the rhythm of Barth's writing in the "small print" sections of the *Dogmatics,* which are (sometimes very long) parenthetical asides where he either exegetes Scripture or engages historical theologies and figures on the point being addressed in the dogmatic exposition of the "big print" sections. In *Dogmatics* I/1, for example, Barth will first show how what he is saying about the Word of God cuts against what he sees as Roman Catholic efforts to control it on any given doctrinal point under discussion, then show how it cuts against modern liberal theology's attempt to control it (again, as he sees it), then against the attempts of conservative evangelical pietism, etc.

12. See, for example, Barth, *Dogmatics* I/1, 162–86. See especially: "Invariably, then, faith is acknowledgment of our limit and acknowledgment of the mystery of God's Word . . . that our hearing is bound to God Himself . . . not giving Himself . . . into our hands but keeping us in His hands" (Barth, *Dogmatics* I/1, 176). See also: The Word of God "presents and places itself as an object over against us . . . [an] object which can never in any sense be our possession" (Barth, *Dogmatics* I/1, 91); God's judgment "cannot be anticipated and never passes under our control" (Barth, *Dogmatics* I/1, 93); "If a man, the Church, Church proclamation and dogmatics think they can handle the Word and faith like capital at their disposal, they simply prove thereby that they have neither the Word nor faith. When we have them, we do not regard them as a possession . . ." (Barth, *Dogmatics* I/1, 225).

And here is the *really* tricky bit. For Barth, the desire and attempt to protect the gospel from what he sees as the ever-present threat of natural theology *is itself always in danger of becoming the move of natural theology.* It succumbs to this danger whenever we assume that we possess the criteria—as something available to our initiative, spontaneity, and agency, and so at our disposal—for judging the goodness of the gospel news. It is inevitable that we engage in natural theology because we quite naturally want to preserve and protect the goodness of the gospel as a life-giving word. Consequently, Barth's theology itself becomes natural theology when written or seized upon as a guarantee of our faithfulness, as securing our knowledge of God and the world, as grounding the right and true interpretation of the gospel and its goodness, as a stronghold against the idolatries of both conservative and progressive theologies—that is, as a stronghold against all forms of natural theology.[13]

Ultimately, for Barth, the criteria for and the guarantor of the goodness of the gospel does not belong to us (including Barth's own theology). It is not at our disposal or under our control. The only criteria for and guarantor of the goodness of the gospel is the Word of God itself—say it with me: the one eternal divine will, decision, Word, and act in which God is wholly and irrevocably for the creature in Jesus (through the Spirit), the last first—to which the gospel points. That is, the criteria for and guarantor of the goodness of the gospel must be given in and with the event of God's free act of self-giving and self-disclosure to the creature, and so always must be *from God*.[14] The

---

13. See, for example: ". . . we must accept the fact that only the Logos of God Himself can provide the proof that we are really talking about Him when we are allegedly doing so. And we should have succumbed already to the afore-mentioned temptation [to master the Word of God] if we were to look about for some means to ward it [the temptation to mastery over the Word] off . . . For it would be a highly refined way of becoming master of God's Word to think we could put ourselves in a position in which we have securely adopted the right attitude to it [e.g., via Barth's theology], that of servant and not master" (Barth, *Dogmatics* I/1, 163). See also: "But on occasions *when* dialectic utterance [e.g., Barth's dialectical method] has seemed to succeed in doing so [bearing witness] . . . it was not because of what the dialectician did . . . but because . . . the living Truth . . . the reality of God, asserted *itself* . . . This possibility . . . that God himself speaks when he is spoken of, is not part of the dialectic way as such . . . In this respect the dialectician [i.e., the Barthian theologian] is no better than the dogmatician and the self-critic . . ." (Barth, "Task of Ministry," 210–11).

14. See, for example: "The Word of God is the judgment in virtue of which alone proclamation can be real proclamation . . . What is to decide this? What is the criterion here? . . . even though it is not known to anyone, a different criterion from these others has given itself to be known . . . this criterion *which we do not know now, or know only from this recollection, will give itself to be known again.* This criterion . . . though not at our disposal

gospel is the news of God's self-giving to the creature becoming actual in Jesus (through the Spirit). Both the criteria for recognizing this event and the guarantor of the goodness of this event are simply the event itself occurring and becoming actual—not simply as a past event (i.e., two thousand years ago in Palestine), but as a living event of personal relation and encounter that is always occurring anew, *from God*, in the power of the Spirit. Consequently, it is not ours to hold and to wield, but only to receive and respond in the moment of the event of divine self-giving and self-disclosure—and only *for* and *in* that moment. It does not pass into our permanent possession.

Barth Is Our Friend Only as Worthy Adversary

This is complicated counterintuitive stuff, and we will unpack it as we move through the coming chapters. At this point, it is enough to recognize that Barth, if we are reading him well, must always be considered as the loyal opposition, as it were, even—or *especially*—when reading him generously as a positive theological resource. If and when he is doing his job rightly, and if and when we are reading him well, all of our best desires and efforts to secure, retrieve, upgrade, or liberate the goodness of the gospel are brought under judgment, shown to be born of our insatiable need for security, certainty, and control (which, for Barth—in resonance with progressives, here—is always one slippery half-step from domination and so destructive bad news for the neighbor and creation).

If and when we are reading Barth well—and when he is being faithful to his fundamental insights, convictions, and commitments—we will be acutely and painfully aware of how and why he is continually pulling the rug out from under our attempts to anchor theological truth and meaning in our best work, in our highest hope, in our most transformative creativity, in our most conservative doctrine, in our most progressive ethics, and most of all, in our most *fideistic Barthianism*. Ergo, the first word of Barth's no to natural theology: Woe to you, self-assured Barthians!

---

in our own or any present, is the Word of God. We cannot 'handle' this criterion. It is the criterion which handles itself and is in no other hands" (Barth, *Dogmatics* I/1, 92–93); "But to say 'God with us' is to say something which has no basis or possibility outside of itself, which can in no sense be explained in terms of man and man's situation, but only as knowledge of God *from God* . . . The *Deus dixit* is true . . . where it is true, i.e., where and when God, in speaking once and for all, wills according to His eternal counsel that it be true" (Barth, *Dogmatics* I/1, 119–20; my emphasis). See also: ". . . the Word of God alone answers the question of real knowledge of the Word of God . . ." (Barth, *Dogmatics* I/1, 189).

WHAT ABOUT THE DIVINE NO OF WRATH, JUDGMENT, AND CONDEMNATION?

Finally, we cannot discuss Barth's belief in the unqualified goodness of the news about Jesus (in the Spirit) without saying something more about all the very obvious bad news about God's wrath and judgment and condemnation that seems to be clearly spelled out in the Bible. This is especially important as Barth claims to take the Bible seriously as the authoritative (albeit human) guide for all that is said and done in and by the church. We are not allowed to simply skip or delete the parts of the biblical witness we don't like, that we find uncomfortable or offensive.

I will just say two things here, as a preface to the treatment of these issues throughout the rest of the book. First, for Barth, whatever very real peril we are in, whatever shadow of divine wrath, judgment, and condemnation we live under as sinners, it can never be the *absolute* peril of *eternal* divine wrath, judgment, and condemnation.[15] God has decided against this possibility concretely and once for all in the divine-human history that is God for us in Jesus (through the Spirit). This is Karl Barth 101, a pivotal signpost. If this is not first and foremost in one's mind or on the table in any reading of or discussion of Barth, he—or at least his *intention*—is not being read well nor sufficiently understood. Whatever divine No one encounters in the biblical witness or in Barth's theology, with all its accompanying danger and threat, it has already, from before the foundations of the world, been strictly limited and finally overcome in the eternal Yes of God to and for the creature that *occurs in* and *is* Jesus Christ (in the Spirit). In this light, the divine No is ultimately a signpost pointing us to gratitude and joy, not fear. It can only point to the unadulterated, unqualified goodness of the news; it cannot compromise or limit it. If this is ever in doubt, up for grabs, looks like it could go either way, the cause for insecurity or anxiety or alarm, if there is ever a sliver of shadow suggesting that God is not wholly for the creature from first to last and that this divine Yes is our—each and every one's—beginning and end,

---

15. See, for example, Barth, *Dogmatics* II/2, 315–25. See especially: "What man can do with his negative act can only be the admittedly real and evil and fatal recollection and reproduction of that which has been removed from him . . . He can certainly flee from God (he does so); but he cannot escape Him" (Barth, *Dogmatics* II/2, 317); "Their concern is still the suffering of the existence which they have prepared for themselves by their godlessness . . . Their concern is still to be aware of the threat of their rejection. But it cannot now be their concern *to suffer the execution of this threat*, to suffer the eternal damnation which their godlessness deserves" (Barth, *Dogmatics* II/2, 319; my emphasis).

then we are not dealing with Barth's understanding of the biblical witness to divine wrath, judgment, and condemnation and its place in the gospel.[16]

Second, in the context of the gospel, as the good news about God's eternal Yes to the creature and creation concretely enacted and accomplished in Jesus (through the Spirit), God's wrath, judgment, and condemnation is not directed at nor does it mean the destruction of sinners. It is directed at and means the destruction of that which holds the beloved sinner in its destructive grip: the power of sin and death. It is not appointed to the destruction of creation or the sinful creature. It is appointed to the destruction of that which is destructive of creation and the sinful creature, for the sake of their salvation. Divine wrath, judgment, and condemnation are not to be seen as opposed to or limiting or sitting alongside and balanced over-against God's salvation of creation and the sinful creature, as if salvation and judgment are two separate and opposed wills in God.[17] For many of us, again, this is counterintuitive theological logic, as the opposing of salvation and judgment as two separate wills in God is as essential to traditional Wesleyan pietism as it is to the classic form of Calvinist double predestination. The only difference is that, in the former, the execution of divine judgment is the result of our decision, and in the latter, it is the result of God's decision. In both cases, the gospel is not the gospel without someone burning in hell for all eternity at the end of the story.[18]

For Barth, God's wrath, judgment, and condemnation of sin *accomplishes* the salvation of creation and the sinful creature by *freeing* the creature and creation from the power of sin. The wrathful divine No of judging and condemning sin *serves* and *accomplishes* the salvific divine Yes to fellowship

---

16. See, for example: "In any case . . . the final word is never that of warning, of judgment, or punishment, of a barrier erected, of a grave opened . . . The Yes cannot be heard unless the No is heard. But the No is said for the sake of the Yes and not for its own sake. In substance, therefore, the first and last word is Yes and not No" (Barth, *Dogmatics* II/2, 13); "On the other hand, if it is the shadow which really predominates, if we must still fear, or if we can only half rejoice and half fear . . . then it is quite certain that we can never again receive or proclaim as such the Gospel previously declared" (Barth, *Dogmatics* II/2, 14).

17. See, for example, Barth, *Dogmatics* II/2 145–94. See especially: ". . . while the will of God in the election of Jesus Christ is indeed double it is not dual. It is not a will directed equally towards man's life and man's death, towards salvation and its opposite" (Barth, *Dogmatics* II/2, 171); "We are no longer free, then, to think of God's eternal election as bifurcating into a rightward and a leftward election. There is a leftward election. But God willed that the object of this election should be Himself and not man" (Barth, *Dogmatics* II/1, 172).

18. For a more in-depth explication of Barth's critical relation to both Reformed and Wesleyan/pietist versions of American evangelicalism on this point, see Boesel, "Better News," 162–90.

and communion with the creature by delivering that creature from the self-destructiveness of sin and into that fellowship and communion. God does not choose to save some sinners while judging and condemning all others. God saves *all* sinners by judging and condemning the sin to which all sinners are held captive.

Finally, then, the Yes and the No in Barth's theology (another one of the more well-known features of his work): the divine Yes always entails a bracketed, limited divine No while remaining, first and last, Yes and only Yes. The goodness of the news about Jesus (in the Spirit) does entail divine wrath, judgment, and condemnation without ceasing to be wholly and unqualifiedly good news for the creature—yea, including and especially the sinful creature—and for all of creation. We will be revisiting these themes of the goodness of the gospel news in relation to the creaturely no to God's unequivocal and irreversible Yes in Jesus (through the Spirit), and the limited nature and status of the biblical witness to the divine No of wrath, judgment, and condemnation, in the following chapters.

QUESTIONS

1. What is the good news, for Barth? How and why is the good news of the gospel wholly and unqualifiedly good?

2. How does Barth's Christocentrism (i.e., Jesus Christ as the one thing churches and Christians have to hear, believe, say, and do) guarantee this goodness of the gospel news, at least from his point of view? How might Barth's Christocentrism be seen to threaten, limit, or undermine the goodness of the Christian message, for example, from more theologically liberal and progressive points of view? Where do you and/or your faith community stand in this disagreement, and why?

3. What is Barth's broad understanding of natural theology? Why does he see it as a threat and limit to the goodness of the gospel news? Can you identify examples of what Barth would call natural theology in your own context and experience? Do you agree with his assessment? Why or why not?

4. How can Barth affirm the biblical witness to divine wrath and judgment and still say that the news is wholly and unqualifiedly good, ultimately not Yes and No, but only Yes? (The following chapters provide further material pertinent to this question. I suggest keeping it in mind as you continue to read.)

PART 2

THE METHOD, LOGIC, AND CONTENT OF BARTH'S THEOLOGY

How Are We Supposed to Do Theology and What Should It Say (and Not Say)?

3

NEITHER OUR POSSESSION NOR AT OUR DISPOSAL

The Break with Liberal Theology,
the Turn to the Bible, and Encountering
an Unknown God

ONE CANNOT UNDERSTAND THE whence and whither of Barth's singular commitment to the one eternal Word of God that is God with and for us in Jesus (through the Spirit)—and with it the major methodological decisions and thematic assertions of his theology, either early or late—without some understanding of the historical context in which Barth's theological vision emerged and the theological assumptions against which he labored for his entire career.[1] The historical context: Europe just prior to, during, and in the aftermath of the First World War. The theological context: what is commonly referred to as the liberal theology of the nineteenth and early twentieth centuries. This theology, internally diverse yet marked by some key shared themes and methodological assumptions, was rooted in the European Enlightenment, nurtured in the rationalism of Kant, and brought to full bloom in the Romanticism of Schleiermacher.[2]

---

1. For a seminal study of the development of Barth's theological vision, see McCormack, *Critically Realistic Dialectical Theology*.

2. For a good introduction to the rise of the modern concept of religion and the corresponding academic disciplines, see Capps, *Religion*, 1–52.

Looking briefly at this context will also give us a sense of why and how a distinctive turn to Scripture became not only central to Barth's theological method and vision throughout his career, but functioned then as now as a key shibboleth that cuts both ways on the theological spectrum, cutting left against liberal and progressive theologies and cutting right against many conservative and traditional theologies. In short, Barth is too conservative for liberals and too liberal for conservatives largely because of his position on and engagement with the Bible.

THE BREAK WITH LIBERAL THEOLOGY

Why did Barth break with liberal theology early in his career? Indeed, this break can be said to have *launched* his career, at least as a professional theologian. Barth was educated in the liberal theology of the nineteenth century. He studied under some of its leading figures. What went wrong? What was so awful that Barth felt a radical break was required? I'll say a few things about liberal theology before turning to Barth's break and his reasons for it.

To read and understand Barth well—that is, not only generously, but also critically—one must be sure to give the liberal theology of his historical context a fair shake and acknowledge its gifts and compelling power (at least for self-consciously "cultured" Western Europeans). One of the limits of Barth's own work is his failure to have made this clear himself on a consistent basis.[3] If one relies solely on Barth for one's knowledge of nineteenth-century liberal theology, one is in danger of getting a very one-sided and ultimately unfair impression.

As Barth himself acknowledged, alas all too rarely, liberal theology was a much-needed corrective to some very real problems with traditional

---

3. There are some exceptions. See, for example: "Whatever one may think of the presuppositions, methods, and results of these nineteenth-century evangelical theologians, it as an act of intellectual and . . . spiritual steadfastness that they were not afraid to face this modern man . . . they dared to expose themselves to this climate as they carried through their work. This work and achievement must be seen and acknowledged" (Barth, "Evangelical Theology," 16); "They wrestled with the challenging issues of their times. Theology—and this was its strength—exposed itself to the world . . . The lazy man may learn thereby what openmindedness is! In this respect evangelical theology of the nineteenth century set an example never to be ignored in any vital theology" (Barth, "Evangelical Theology," 18). See also: "The only certain consolation which remains for me is to rejoice that in the kingdom of heaven I will be able to discuss all these questions with Schleiermacher extensively . . . for, let us say, a couple of centuries. 'Then I will see clearly that—along with so many other things, also that—which on earth I saw through a glass darkly.' I can imagine that that will be a very serious matter for both sides, but also that we will both laugh very heartily at ourselves" (Barth, *Theology of Schleiermacher*, 277).

Christianities. (a) *Epistemologically*, traditional Christianities were in a reactionary and defensive position in relation to the overwhelming developments in philosophy and the sciences, developments that were accompanied by a radical shift of cultural power and authority away from the church and toward cultural institutions rooted more and more in philosophy and the sciences. This tended to put the church in a closed, hostile posture in relation to the world it is called to love and to serve. (b) *Theologically*, this resulted in the image of an increasingly judgmental, uncaring, and exclusionary Christian God and church. (c) *Ethically*, the requirement of unquestioning fealty to the authorities of the church and/or of Scripture was increasingly experienced as coercive and repressive amidst the fast-growing belief in the freedom of conscience and of the individual (at least the white, propertied, male individual). This was accompanied by a growing critique of the socio-political power of church structures and hierarchies as unwarranted, anachronistic, and obstructionist in relation to the advancement of the social good (again, as seen from a so-called cultured Eurocentric-colonial viewpoint).[4]

In this context, liberal theology can be seen to offer a compelling alternative. It confirms as the central truth of Christianity that a beneficent relation of fundamental unity between God, creation, and the human being is indeed the ground of all things and of all meaning, and that the person and history of Jesus is somehow central to the full flowering of this relation and its goodness. However, this affirmation departed from traditional Christian theology in four key ways. First, this relation is assumed to be wholly given in and with nature, and so fundamentally anthropological, rooted in the constitution of the human being qua human—in our reason or in an innate religious capacity, or both, and therefore universal and equally available to all (but not *really* all; again, given the Eurocentric-colonial and patriarchal assumptions at work; more on these necessary qualifications in the last chapter)—rather than uniquely and miraculously in the person of Jesus. Second, the obstacle preventing this relation from determining our entire creaturely reality—i.e., the kingdom of God on earth—is our ignorance of this reality, rather than a catastrophic and irreversible rupture in our relation to the divine caused by willful rebellion, i.e., original sin. Third, the centrality of Jesus is as a paradigm and exemplar of what, in principle, every human being and

---

4. One way in which Barth himself remained "liberal"—or more accurately, progressive—throughout his career was in his conviction that the content of the gospel looked much more like socialism than capitalism in the flesh of socio-economic reality. He remained a card-carrying though critical socialist, and a harsh critic of capitalism, throughout his life. For essays on Barth's relation to progressive politics, see Hunsinger, *Barth and Radical Politics*.

every society can become—i.e., fully realized human potential as a natural human possibility—by fulfilling our natural human potential through full awareness of our true reality as naturally grounded in the divine and so in unity with each other and with all that is. Fourth, even while Jesus functions as paradigm and exemplar, the proper and most reliable access to the knowledge, understanding, and development of this relation to the divine is located where the supreme instance of that relation is most readily and generally to be found: the natural constitution of the (again: white, propertied, male) human creature, as a fundamentally rational and/or religious creature. Knowledge of God begins and ends with knowledge of ourselves (again: white, male, . . .), given that the very constitution of our being is the conduit for our connection with the divine and with ultimate reality. Anthropology (as a Western academic discipline governed by white, male . . .) is the gateway to theology.

What's not to like (if you happen to be white, male, propertied, . . .)? Christian faith on these terms puts everyone (again: *if* white, male, . . .) on an equal footing. *All* (again: *if* . . . ; we can never be reminded often enough) have equal access to both the knowledge and reality of the God-relation that is the ground of all that is, simply by being human. God is equally related—equally close and equally distant, equally mysterious—to *all* (again: . . .). In one fell swoop, gone is the authority of anachronistic ideas over one's own conscience; the arbitrary hierarchical power structures of the church; the unethical exclusionary and judgmental relations between Christianity and other religions and cultures—at least in principle, at least from the Eurocentric, colonialist perspective. Despite varying methods and content across nineteenth-century liberal theologies, there is a recognizable shared vision: everyone (again: . . .) has equal access to divine reality and ultimate truth via the natural endowments of reason and/or religious capacity. As a consequence, each one is their own authority in matters of conscience and religion and is therefore free from all external, coercive, and exclusionary authorities or powers. The intention of early liberal theology can only be rightly understood when heard in the context of Kant's exhilarating call to liberation from the tyranny of superstition and all arbitrary external authority: liberate yourself from your self-incurred tutelage and think for yourself![5] (Again: *if* . . .)

Liberal theology understood itself as delivering a modern, relevant Christianity that was not only more reasonable, but more *fair*—indeed, more just—than traditional Christianity. Again, in principle. (And again: quite explicitly *not*, in fact, for *all*.)

---

5. "*Sapere aude!* 'Have the courage to use your own reason!'—that is the motto of the enlightenment" (Kant, "What Is Enlightenment?," 85).

As with all things, the stirring desire of early liberal theology to liberate (those recognized to be included fully in) humanity from its self-incurred tutelage—a bondage that included the many very real problems with traditional Christianity—was significantly flawed. Barth is not the only one to come to this judgment. Inheritors of the liberal theological tradition itself, now doing the work of various contemporary progressive theologies, are also quite critical of early liberal theology, largely in response to the vanguard of diverse liberation theologies and their prophetic critiques.[6] Most obviously, as my parenthetical commentary has continually reminded us, liberal theology was rooted in unexamined assumptions about race, gender, and class—but also sexuality and ability—such that the "everyone" of "humanity" embraced so stirringly in its vision was radically and rather obviously limited to educated and economically privileged white Anglo-European men.

It must be said that, for most progressive and liberation theologians making this critical judgment upon early liberal theology, Barth himself fairs no better on this score. He is among those privileged, male, European voices from which Christian theology and faith must be liberated if it is indeed to have a good word for the world. Taking the various versions of this critical judgment of Barth seriously, together with providing resources for understanding Barth that assist the reader in coming to their own assessment on these issues, is a central goal of this introductory companion to Barth's work. (While a concern throughout, and behind two of my stylistic conventions in rendering Barth's understanding of what is included in the one Word that is Jesus Christ, this will be the focus of chapters 6 and 7.)

That said, let us look briefly at what Barth came to find problematic about liberal theology despite its compelling assessment (at least for many privileged Anglo-Europeans) of the problems of traditional Christianity and the institutional church—problems of which, it must be said, Barth himself (in cutting to the right) never ceased to be critical. That is to say, to fully understand Barth's critique of liberal theology, one must see how and why Barth was neither defending nor endorsing traditional theologies and forms of church polity and practice in their various orthodoxies for their own sake or in principle. Barth's theology contains its own serious critiques of theological traditions when and where Barth feels it is warranted, critiques that can resonate quite strongly with many of the concerns of liberal and progressive theologies, both yesterday and today (as well as with, I will argue,

---

6. See, for example, feminist theology from Mary Daly to Elizabeth Johnson, eco theology from Sallie McFague to Catherine Keller, Black liberation theology from James Cone to Willie Jennings, Womanist theology from Audre Lorde to Kelly Brown Douglas, queer theology from Carter Heyward to Linn Marie Tonstad.

a progressive ethics—that is, when judged and corrected by the voices of liberation theologies and the experiences, hopes, and visions of the communities from which they emerge).

Court Prophets and the *Gott mit Uns!*

Barth's bitter disappointment at what he saw as a radical failure in the crisis of the First World War is probably the most well-known explanation for why Barth broke with liberal theology and its leading advocates and practitioners.[7] All the leading German figures of the liberal theologies of the day officially signed their names to the Kaiser's war effort. This was not a failure in Barth's eyes because he was a pacifist (he was not) or had a different view on the justness of this particular war (he did). The failure was ultimately *theological* for Barth.

For Barth, the endorsement of the Kaiser's war declaration by virtually the entire liberal theology establishment in Germany revealed the absence of any prophetic voice with critical distance from and leverage over-against both the national culture and the crown.[8] There was no distance between the Christian faith and theology of the liberal church and the spirit of the people, the nation, the *Volk*, as expressed in cultural institutions and traditions and the various national and cultural corridors of power. Perhaps without intending to, liberal theology appeared to be uniquely suited for creating what in the narratives of the Hebrew Bible are called "court prophets"—"yes men" (and in both the Hebrew Bible and modern liberal theology, it is a pretty safe bet that we are talking exclusively of men) to the principalities and powers, to the prevailing winds, be they the whims of the crown or the spirit of the age and its cultural achievements. Barth felt a necessary and urgent question pressing upon him: Where were the Elijahs, the Jeremiahs, the Amoses, bringing a word from God—from *outside* the court, the temple, the market place, and the public square—a word of warning and woe to the crown, the priests, and the people celebrating in the high cultural and political places? Certainly, the crisis of the First World War was a time for the churches in Germany to exercise their prophetic vocation. Alas, the ubiquitous *Gott mit uns!* of German war propaganda became, for Barth, whether fairly or unfairly, the signature theological achievement of liberal theology.

7. *Gott mit uns*, German for "God with us," was a war slogan used in Germany during the First and Second World Wars.

8. Barth himself was Swiss, but he was trained in the German university system, by predominantly German scholars and theologians, some of which were quite well known, including Adolf Harnack and Wilhelm Herrmann.

In light of this *Gott mit uns!* we can see how the assumption of a natural continuity, if not identity, between the human and the divine, itself a remedy for traditional Christianity's toxically harsh and judgmental *distance* between God and humanity, now appeared to cast its own, albeit unintended, problematic shadow, a shadow calling out for a remedy. Liberal theology's version of Christianity's supposedly good news—"God with us!"—was found without resources to resist, or to even feel the need to resist, its co-option by the crown and the spirit of the *Volk* in the *Gott mit us!* of Germany's war propaganda. From Barth's point of view, he did not set out to bring down liberal theology; he woke up to find it bankrupt and in pieces among the rubble and ruins of Europe at war.

Red Pastor: Jesus and Socialism

The First World War is an important part of the story, but it is not the whole story. Before the advent of the war, Barth was already becoming dissatisfied with the liberal theology in which he had been educated. Upon completing his studies, Barth took up a position as a pastor in the Swiss industrial town of Safenwil. His congregation was predominately made up of factory workers and their families. He quickly became sympathetic to the economic hardships of the poor and working classes. He became more aware of the disparity in living conditions between the poor and working classes and the middle class, and more critical of the economic structures of capitalism that appeared to create that disparity and hold it intractably in place. Informed by the work of certain Christian socialists, Barth became more and more active in advocating for the basic dignity and security of his proletariat parishioners.[9] He became known as the Red Pastor of Safenwil, publically announcing things like, "*Real* socialism is real Christianity in our time" (with the qualifier "real" in both cases signifying important qualifications, of course).[10]

During this time, Barth came to see the mainstream of liberal theology as primarily a middle class and so a socially and politically *conservative* phenomenon. The innate continuity it fashioned between the divine Spirit and the human spirit tended to recognize itself more in the institutions, expressions, and productions known as "high culture," institutionally grounded and

---

9. Particularly influential on Barth's theological thinking about socialism, Leonhard Ragaz (1868–1945) and Hermann Kutter (1863–1931) were the founders of religious socialism in Switzerland.

10. See Barth, "Jesus and Social Justice," 36. In this lecture, Barth describes the movement of Jesus as "entirely a *movement from below*," language that became a standard slogan of liberation theologies fifty years later (Barth, "Jesus and Social Justice," 23).

economically supported by existing social, economic, and political forces favorable to the middle and upper classes.[11] This created a cultural and political conservativism whereby being a good Christian became synonymous with being a good citizen of Western culture, supporting and consuming the fruits of its cultural expressions and productions and the existing economic and institutional structures that made them possible, including the structures of "law and order" that kept a repressive lid on the political activities and social aspirations of the working classes that were seen to threaten the comforts of the *status quo*. Like Kierkegaard before him, and liberation theologians after him, Barth became increasingly convinced that this kind of comfortable Christianity, at home and content with the best that Western civilization has to offer, had very little to do with the poor Jew from Nazareth who had not a stone upon which to lay his head, who was tortured and executed by the state as a criminal threat to law and order, rejected by both the religious authorities and "the crowd." Robert Perkins's summary of Kierkegaard's critique of Bishop Mynster, the preeminent liberal pastor and theologian of mid-nineteenth-century Denmark, is apt here: The bishop was wealthy, Jesus was poor; the bishop was an official of the state, Jesus was executed by the state; the bishop was respected in society, Jesus was rejected by society.[12]

Barth ultimately became severely critical of socialism itself—or more accurately, of the socialist parties across Europe. In the crisis of the First World War, socialist parties consistently betrayed the central socialist commitment to international solidarity among workers and the rejection of all nationalisms. Socialists by and large capitulated to their respective nationalisms and enlisted in their various national armies to fight and kill each other all across Europe. As disappointing as this was, Barth never broke his affiliation with socialism, particularly in the face of the going alternative: capitalism. His disillusionment with socialism was due to the failure of the socialist parties across Europe to be socialist *enough*. And for the young Barth, the failure of socialism to be socialist enough meant that the extant socialisms across Europe also failed to keep pace with the radicality of a truly *Christian* socio-political vision, at least as he understood it. It goes without saying that the churches—with both their conservative and liberal theologies, ecclesiologies, and practices—had already failed miserably in this respect, which is why

---

11. See, for example: "How long did it take the Church to become concerned about social questions, to take socialism seriously . . . How naively did the Church subscribe to political conservatism in the first half of the century and in the second half to the preservation of the liberal bourgeoisie, the growing nationalism and militarism" (Barth, "Evangelical Theology," 27–28).

12. Perkins, *Kierkegaard*, 7.

Barth initially had high hopes for the promise of socialism as heralding the advent of the in-breaking of the kingdom of God known in Jesus (though the Spirit). (We will have more to say about Barth and socialism in the last chapter.)

In both of these cases—the First World War and the liberative vision of socialism—liberal theology's remedy for the very real distortions of traditional Christianity's various versions of "God with us" failed to retrieve and secure the goodness of this news. The assumption of a natural continuity between God and ourselves and our cultures (at least as conceived by and for privileged, cultured Europeans)—i.e., the parts of ourselves and our cultures we are especially proud of, the intellectually, ethically, and aesthetically sophisticated and accomplished parts, the good parts, the "high" parts—turned out to be extremely problematic. In his discernment of the signs and spirits of the age, Barth concluded that the destructive consequences of the First World War and of capitalism, both of which were concurrent with the cultural triumph of liberal theology, demonstrated ample evidence that there was indeed no such continuity.

This was the predicament Barth discovered himself to be in during the second decade of the twentieth century. What's a pastor and theologian to do in such a situation? Where to turn? What alternatives presented themselves?

One thing Barth did *not* do was to become a conservative reactionary and retreat to the cold comforts of Protestant orthodoxy, though this is often how he is perceived and portrayed. The well-known yet ill-fitting label of neo-orthodoxy that is often applied to Barth implies that he did just this.[13] However, the problems of traditional Christianites that liberal theology was trying to remedy did not disappear or become more attractive in light of what Barth judged to be the latter's catastrophic failure. Neither did Barth give up

---

13. The label "neo-orthodoxy" is misleading in relation to Barth if it means, as it does for many, that Barth uncritically reclaimed and reaffirmed both the authority and the theological content of the Protestant Reformers in an attempt to take the church "back" to the theology of the sixteenth century as the only alternative to modern liberal theology. Yes, Barth "went back to" and "rediscovered" the Reformers in many ways—particularly in their own "going back" to hear the biblical witness anew, with a prophetic, critical edge in relation to church authority—and mined much of what became Protestant orthodoxy in the seventeenth and eighteenth centuries. But this was *productive* for Barth, rather than an act of retrieval, preservation, or repetition. It opened up a way forward, not backward; a way forward that included his own severe critiques the Reformation traditions in the name of what he thought he heard as the biblical witness to the gospel. What he learned most from the Reformers was the prophetic critique of the biblical witness over against all church theology, including what became the Protestant orthodoxies spawned by those very Reformers.

on the Christian "God with us," nor on the hope that its promise was indeed life-giving and affirming good news and not death-dealing bad news, and that its life-giving and affirming goodness was for all, the last, first, without limit or qualification, including the qualifications the church was endlessly coming up with to both possess and diminish (even in its efforts to protect and guarantee) that goodness. The answer, at least for Barth, was not "God *against* us" (though Barth would appear to say something very close to this in the early days of his break with liberal theology), nor a God of indifference, nor the conclusion that there is no God at all, despite the fact that these were all compelling alternatives amidst the rubble and ruin of Europe circa 1918.

So, again, what to do? Where to turn? Where to begin thinking again about the Christian "God with us" as a European pastor amidst the rubble and ruin of Europe and of liberal theology? One thing was clear to Barth: Liberal theology's decision to begin with general anthropology, with a philosophical or scientific knowledge of ourselves and our experience, generally available to us through natural and historical resources and processes—i.e., its decision to commit itself wholly to a modern form of natural theology—had proved a blind alley.[14] Another beginning, a different methodological starting place was needed.

STRANGE NEW WORLD WITHIN THE BIBLE

This is the context in which Barth—together with his good friend, Eduard Thurneysen—turns to the Bible in his break with liberal theology.[15] There are a handful of important points about this turn that the context of the failed promise of liberal theology (at least as Barth saw it) amidst the rubble of Europe enables us to see.

First, Barth's turn to the Bible is a search for a new starting point for faith and for theology. Here was the burning question facing Barth at this

---

14. See, for example: "Theology, however, went overboard . . . insofar as confrontation with the contemporary age was its *decisive* and *primary* concern . . . The winds were enthusiastically welcomed and allowed to enter freely through the outside doors . . . This meant that fatal errors blew in, were admitted, and made themselves at home" (Barth, "Evangelical Theology," 19).

15. The subhead for this section is taken from a chapter in *Word of God, Word of Man*, a collection of some of Barth's early lectures and addresses, from 1916 to 1923. For Barth's theological relationship with Thurneysen, see Smart, *Revolutionary Theology*. For Thurneysen's version of what Barth calls the imperative entailed in the indicative ("Be what you already are in grace!"), and the counterintuitive idea of free creaturely obedience as response to the gospel of radical grace (see ch. 6), see also Thurneysen, *Sermon on the Mount*.

time: *If* pastors and theologians, and the church more generally, are to know and to speak of God with any assurance that we are truly speaking of God when we attempt to do so and not only of ourselves, where do we begin?[16] To what do we turn for the proper foundation for such knowledge and speaking? For theology, this is a methodological and an epistemological question. What do we do first, in order to set us upon the path of actual knowledge of God that is not simply knowledge of ourselves in fancy dress speaking in a deep and loud voice?[17]

Second, this turn to the Bible as a possible new, alternative starting point for knowledge of God that is not simply knowledge of ourselves in disguise is made out of desperation, in a predicament of bankruptcy and impoverishment, out of a sense of having nowhere else to turn. It is not made in the confident assurance that this was the right move, the appropriate remedy, with a clear, self-assured understanding that the error of liberal theology was its *turning away* from the Bible, and so now the appropriate remedy is a *return to* the Bible. The turn to the Bible was not made as a return to the old sources and old answers and old assurances. It was not undertaken as a retreat. It was undertaken as an advance into new and unknown territory.[18]

Barth and Thurneysen, having been educated and formed in and by liberal theology, picked up the Bible with a healthy modern skepticism, with no certain confidence that they would find anything but the old and archaic, the anachronistic and irrelevant. But they were desperate. What they thought they knew lay in rubble and ash at their feet. One can imagine the conversation over a couple steins down at the pub:

16. See, for example: "Our difficulty lies in the content of our task . . . *As ministers we ought to speak of God. We are human, however, and so cannot speak of God. We ought therefore to recognize both our obligation and our inability and by that very recognition give God the glory*" (Barth, "Task of Ministry," 186).

17. This is Barth's snarky jab: "With all due respect to the genius shown in his work, I can *not* consider Schleiermacher a good teacher in the realm of theology because . . . he is disastrously dim-sighted in regard to the fact that man as man is not only in *need* but beyond all hope of saving himself; that the whole of so-called religion, and not least the Christian religion, *shares* in this need; and that one can *not* speak of God simply by speaking of man in a loud voice" (Barth, "Task of Ministry," 195).

18. See, for example: "The question, What is within the Bible? . . . we must . . . reach eagerly for an answer which is really much too large for us, for which we really are not yet ready . . . since it is a fruit which our own longing, striving, and inner labor have not planted . . . within the Bible there is a strange, new world, the world of God" (Barth, "Strange New World," 32); "[I]n the Bible, in both the Old and the New Testaments, the theme is . . . the religion of God and never once the religion of the Jews, or Christians, or heathen . . . in this respect, as in others, the Bible lifts us out of the old atmosphere of man to the open portals of a new world, the world of God" (Barth, "Strange New World," 45).

So now what?

I know it sounds crazy, but what about reading the Bible?

Why not? We've run out of options.

What have we got to lose?

So they begin reading Paul's Letter to the Romans.

Third, what happened then was that *something happened*. This desperate experiment, this grasping at straws, turned into what generous readers of Barth now look back on as his and Thurneysen's prescient "turn to the Bible." But it only looks prescient in hindsight. At the time, they turned to the Bible in the absence of any better ideas or anything better to do, and something happened to them, or at least they *felt* as if something happened to them, something that they could not anticipate. After turning to the Bible, not knowing what they would find, they actually found something, or more accurately, according to their experience (as Barth reports it), something *found them*. They experienced themselves as encountered by something, as hearing something. They felt themselves to be addressed by a voice and a word they did not recognize and did not know.

On an initial level, they experienced themselves being addressed by the Apostle Paul (having begun with Paul's Letter to the Romans). Paul and his letter was no longer the object of their study, as had been the case at university and was the case for liberal theology. Rather, they experienced themselves as the audience of Paul's address.[19] It suddenly seemed to them that it was not the sophistication of their modern historical and philosophical knowledge that enabled an appropriate interpretation of Paul. Rather, it was *Paul* who appeared to know something that they did not know and by which *they* were being interpreted. They felt as if they were not in control of this encounter.

On another level—an ultimately more important and primary level—Paul's address seemed to point away from Paul himself to something else, to someone else.[20] What Paul appeared to know and understand was not his own

---

19. See, for example: "By genuine understanding and interpretation I mean that creative energy which Luther exercised . . . [and] which underlies the systematic interpretation of Calvin . . . how energetically Calvin . . . sets himself to re-think the whole material and to wrestle with it, till the walls which separate the sixteenth century from the first become transparent! Paul speaks, and the man of the sixteenth century hears" (Barth, *Romans*, 7). See also Robinson, "Critical Historical Method."

20. See, for example: "Witnessing means pointing in a specific direction beyond the self and on to another . . . Standing in this service, the biblical witnesses point beyond themselves" (Barth, *Dogmatics* I/1, 111); "[T]he revelation to which the biblical witnesses direct their gaze as they look and point away from themselves is to be distinguished from the word of the witnesses in exactly the same way as an event itself is to be distinguished from even the best and most faithful account of it . . . On one hand *Deus dixit*, on the

possession. It was not something that belonged to him and was therefore his to impart. Rather, what Paul appeared to know—according to Barth's hearing—was where to point; Paul appeared to know to point away from himself and in which direction. What Barth and Thurneysen felt they discovered or had been encountered by in turning to follow the direction of Paul's pointing was a God who was unknown to them. The God of the Bible was suddenly a strange God, a God best described as "wholly other" to the human being.[21]

This God could not be more different than what Barth now saw as the familiar God of liberal theology. The latter was a God who was, in fact, the best version of our own vision of ourselves (as white, male, educated, propertied . . .); whose presence and work in the world was expressed through the highest and best and most refined, most cultured capacities and aspirations of the human project. In reading Paul, what was once so intimately internal to ourselves and the presumed "civilized" cultural life of the West as to be the most natural thing in the world, so intimately known, familiar, safe, domesticated, a benign presence around the family hearth of bourgeois Western culture, had now become a strange and wild, untamed, unpredictable—and to that extent, a quite possibly dangerous—thing.

Suddenly, for Barth, the game was afoot. We are caught up in a drama and a history not of our own making and not answerable to our beck and call—a drama and history not to be determined and decided by our best knowledge and mastery of ourselves and our world. In fact, we are not even the central actor of the story. We are caught up in a story that is not our own. We are awakened, confronted, and addressed, interrogated, called to

---

other *Paulus dixit*. These are two different things." But we must not ignore the immediate sequel: these two things "*become* one and the same thing *in the event* of the Word of God" (Barth, *Dogmatics* I/1, 113; my emphases). See also: "But the activity of the community is related to the Gospel only in so far as it is no more than a crater formed by the explosion of a shell and seeks to be no more than a void in which the Gospel reveals itself. The people of Christ . . . know only those words and works and things which by their negation are sign-posts to the Holy One" (Barth, *Romans*, 36).

21. Barth later acknowledged the one-sidedness of this emphasis on the "unknown God" as "wholly other"—though arguing that it was necessary at the time, given the context—and that it obscured both the full content and goodness of the gospel as news that this God has given Godself to the creature *to be known and loved* in partnership, fellowship, and communion. See, for example: "We viewed this 'wholly other' in isolation, abstracted and absolutized, and set it over against man . . . But did it not appear to escape us by quite a distance that the *deity* of the *living* God—and we certainly wanted to deal with Him—found its meaning and its power only in the context of His history and of His dialogue with *man*, and thus in His *togetherness* with man? . . . in the fact that He exists, speaks, and acts as the *partner* of man, though of course as the absolutely superior partner" (Barth, "Humanity of God," 45).

respond, called to account.[22] We awake to find ourselves neither in the starring role nor in control.

For Barth, this methodological starting point was definitely *not* the starting point of liberal theology. Instead of starting with what was considered to be the most sophisticated and advanced and intimate knowledge of human being—the knowledge accessible to the properly educated and cultured European male—we begin as addressed, interrupted, and interrogated by a God who is "wholly other" to all that we are and know, who is so strange and undomesticated that we cannot but encounter them as threat and even as "enemy" to all that brings us certainty, security, comfort, and order.[23] All that was thought to constitute certainty, security, comfort, and order—at least for the properly educated and cultured European male—now lay among the rubble and ruin of Europe in that historical moment. Barth found himself compelled to consider that this unknown God, who is stranger and threat to all that was considered the best and brightest of European thought and culture, but which could not save Europe from its own self-destruction, perhaps this way of risk, encounter, strangeness, and perceived threat held the promise of life, a rediscovery of the true human situation—at least in the Anglo-European context of life among the ruins.

God as the Unknown "Wholly Other"

Here we encounter another one of those things for which Barth is infamous: the discovery—or the rediscovery—of the radical *transcendence* of God, in distinction from the divine *immanence* in which liberal theology envisioned God as immanent to anthropology, as natural and internal to the human

---

22. This is in keeping with one of Barth's central themes, the reversal in direction of movement in relation to liberal theology: *God seeks, finds, addresses, questions us*, not vice versa. See, for example: "When we come to the Bible with our questions—How shall I think of God and the universe? How arrive at the divine? . . . it answers us, as it were, 'My dear sir, these are your problems: you must not ask *me*! . . . If you do not care to enter upon *my* questions . . . you will not then find what is really here' . . . It is not the right human thoughts about God which form the content of the Bible, but the right divine thoughts about men. The Bible tells us not how we should talk with God but what he says to us; not how we find the way to him, but how he has sought and found the way to us" (Barth, "Strange New World," 42–43; see also n66).

23. See, for example, the following parable: "*On the battlefield* (namely, not in a study . . .) *it has happened* (. . . with the whole gravity of a factual event) *that the enemy* (the enemy, the other one, not man himself but his opponent, an adversary who is determined to engage man) . . . *has gone into action* . . . This event is God's revelation" (Barth, "Revelation," 4).

(albeit white, male, . . .) constitution and experience. The most well-known instance of Barth's view of the radical transcendence of God is his description of "the unknown God" as the "Wholly Other" in his commentary on Romans. However, for Barth, it becomes clear that divine transcendence is not the whole story or even the most important part of the story. The real point of the story for Barth, even in the commentary on Romans, was still the gospel's "God with us," and more and more in the coming decades, God with *and for* us.[24] However, given the theological assumptions determining that particular context, emphasizing the otherness of God certainly seemed like a good idea at the time.

Even those who later became Barth's theological adversaries as twentieth-century liberal theologians—e.g., Paul Tillich and Rudolph Bultmann—initially welcomed Barth's discovery of radical divine transcendence as the promise of a new beginning for Christian theology.[25] These twentieth-century liberal theologians later came to fall out with Barth—and he with them—because they felt he was not staying true to this discovery in his later work. They felt the God of his mature theology—church dogmatics, of all things! (How unsexy can you get?)—was no longer *transcendent enough*. Alternatively, Barth's view was that they did not understand divine transcendence *in the right way*. He felt that they retreated to a *philosophical* (metaphysical, ontological) form of transcendence—for example, Tillich's view of *esse ipsum*: "Being itself," or the Ground of Being, as Christian theology's primary language for God. Barth saw this as ultimately providing cover for sneaking an updated version of liberal theology's divine immanence back in the side door: the divine Ground of Being as ontologically constitutive of all creaturely being. This, as distinct from what Barth understood as the *personal* form of divine transcendence (and immanence)—God's freedom, holiness, righteousness, justice, love, and mercy—that was more characteristic of the biblical witness and which Barth found to be the more radical of the two forms.[26]

---

24. See, for example, the very first page introducing "the theme of the epistle": "The Gospel of the Resurrection is the action, the supreme miracle, by which God, the unknown God dwelling in light unapproachable, the Holy One, Creator, and Redeemer, *makes Himself known*" (my emphasis); and later—"At these crossroads, then, God's own Son stands . . . God sends him—from the realm of the eternal, unfallen, unknown world of the Beginning and the End . . . God sends him—into this temporal, fallen world . . . into this humanity and into this flesh" (Barth, *Romans*, 35, 277).

25. See Green, *Theologian of Freedom*, 18.

26. For more on the difference that personal as distinct from merely metaphysical transcendence makes, see Boesel, "Apophasis of Divine Freedom."

For most late-twentieth-century and early twenty-first-century liberal and progressive theologies, divine transcendence has become a bad word, and Barth's God is now critiqued for being *too* transcendent. However, in the particular context of Barth's initial "turn to the Bible" amidst the ruin and rubble of Europe, this thing that Barth and Thurneysen believed happened to them in reading Paul—the discovery of the transcendence of God in this strange, apostolic piece of news and its radical reorientation of the God-world relation as they knew it—struck them and many of their peers as the needed remedy for and corrective to the apparent failures of liberal theology.[27]

THE BIBLE AS AUTHORITATIVE HUMAN WITNESS

While Barth's turn to the Bible was a pivotal catalyst in the search for a new starting point and foundation for Christian faith and theology, the Bible *itself*, strictly speaking, as we have already seen, is not that starting point or foundation. As mentioned above in reference to Paul, the Bible itself—which Barth liked to refer to as the prophetic and apostolic witness to Jesus Christ—*points to* that starting point and foundation. As with Paul's Letter to the Romans, for Barth, the Bible itself is not the living Word of God such that when we hold the Bible in our hands, we hold the Word of God in our hands. The living Word of God is not identical with the human words constituting the content of the Bible and so is not at our disposal when we read, cite, memorize, and repeat those words. For Barth, the Word of God is never ours to take up and wield according to our judgment, discretion, or desire. Therefore, the Bible must not be approached, held, or read as if it placed the living Word of God into our hands, onto our lips, and under our control in this way. For Barth, as we will continue to see, the Word of God can be spoken by and is the possession of God alone. Consequently, it can only come to us *from God*—from God's own mouth and from God's own hands. We can only hear it and receive it and know it in the free event of God's speaking and acting in Jesus (through the Spirit).

For Barth, the Bible itself is not this event of God's speaking and acting, nor can it, of its own accord, produce this event, nor can *we*, in picking up the

---

27. This, of course, implies that we—especially generous readers of Barth—must always be open to the possibility that what we might still feel is Barth's "perfect remedy" to liberal theology in that context might run up against its own limits and failures that become more visible and obvious in other contexts (e.g., twenty-first century recognition and analysis of colonialism, racism, patri-kyriarchy, sexism, homophobia, heterosexism, ableism, and ecological catastrophe) just as, in Barth's own judgment, liberal theology's "perfect remedy" ran up against its own limits in its own as well as other contexts.

Bible and wielding it through our reading and interpretation and preaching and, least of all, proof texting, produce this event. Rather, Barth describes the Bible as a thoroughly human record of the event of God's speaking and acting as it has occasionally occurred in the commissioned careers of the prophets and the apostles through Israel's journey among the nations.[28] It bears human witness to this event. It recollects this event. *But it is not the event itself.*[29] Yes, Barth believes God has spoken and acted. But the words on the pages of the Bible are wholly and thoroughly human, with all the problematic frailty and risk that entails. There is nothing divine about those words in themselves—often far from it, in fact.

Consequently, in and through Paul's human gesture of pointing in testimony and witness to what he himself claimed to have heard and seen, to what he claimed was his own encounter with an unknown and strange God—an encounter that quite literally knocked him both off and on his respective asses (according to the biblical witness)—Barth and Thurneysen experienced themselves addressed, questioned, and pursued by this God. In Paul's problematic and frail and unreliable human words, they heard themselves—at least according to their own testimonies—addressed by a Word from God's own mouth in a free event of divine self-giving; an event that neither the words of Paul nor their own picking up and reading of those words, their studying, interpreting, preaching, criticizing, or believing in those words could or can produce.

It is this strange, un-anticipatable, and un-producible (i.e., impossible—*for us*)[30] event of divine speaking and acting, then, that Barth discovered as the new starting point and foundation for Christian faith and theology in his turn to the Bible. The Bible itself played an essential role in Barth's particular

---

28. See, for example: "in Holy Scripture . . . the writing is obviously not primary, but secondary. It is itself the deposit of what was once proclamation by human lips . . . Scripture as the commencement and present day preaching as the continuation of one and the same event, Jeremiah and Paul at the beginning and the modern preacher of the Gospel at the end of one and the same series" (Barth, *Dogmatics* I/1, 102); "Holy Scripture is the record of a unique hearing of a unique call . . ." (Barth, *Dogmatics* I/1, 115).

29. See, for example: "The Bible is the concrete means by which the Church recollects God's past revelation, is called to expectation of His future revelation . . . The Bible, then, *is not in itself and as such God's past revelation* . . ." (Barth, *Dogmatics* I/1, 111; my emphasis).

30. Barth often uses the phrase "impossible possibility" to describe the event of revelation, and of faith (as well as the reality of sin). The realities of revelation and faith, which always occur in the nature of an event, are impossible for us, in terms of natural, creaturely constitution, capacity, and possibility. But they are events that nevertheless occur, are actual—and so possible—as works of *divine* possibility, that call forth and enable creaturely response to and participation in those events/realities.

journey to this discovery. But the Bible itself is not this encounter and address, nor does it or can it produce this encounter and address; not for Barth and Thurneysen, and not for us—according to Barth and Thurneysen.[31]

Cutting Both Ways

Barth's turn to the Bible takes on a double edge in relation to the theological alternatives of his day. This double edge characterizes his theology throughout his career and continues to do so in our own time.

On one hand, cutting against liberal and progressive theologies on the left, Barth acknowledges and affirms the (albeit relative) authority of the Bible for Christian faith and theology. Barth describes the Bible in itself—sitting on the table, as it were—as the authoritative human witness to the Word of God for the church.[32] It is the divinely commissioned prophetic and apostolic witness to the "God with and for us" that is eternally willed and concretely actual in Jesus (through the Spirit), that is, to the Word of God that is, for Barth, both the content and criteria of Christian faith and theology. As such, the Bible is to function as the rule and guide for all that is said and done in the church. For Barth, it is not to be identified with the word and work of the church. It confronts the church with a word—and, *if and when* God so wills, a Word in and through this word—that the church did not and cannot create, conjure, or choose; that it does not and cannot know apart from this confrontation and address; and that it still cannot possess or control no matter how many times that word is heard, no matter how many times the Bible is picked up and read, preached, studied, and memorized.

This is much *more* authority than the liberal theologies of the nineteenth and early twentieth century, and the progressive theologies of today, want to give the Bible. Consequently, they can only view Barth as too theologically conservative. From their point of view—and for very good reasons, not without much compelling historical and theological evidence—investing the Bible with too much authority can only be dangerous and destructive, can only distort Christianity into a vehicle for bad and very destructive news (e.g., for women, for LGBTQIA+ folks, for the environment, for unbelievers, and for the cultures and practitioners of other religions). Indeed, the Bible

---

31. And, needless to say, not for Paul, given that the New Testament did not yet exist at the time; he had yet to write most of it. It would seem, then, that the God who is only God as God for us in Jesus Christ (though the Spirit) can show up in person even when there isn't a Bible in sight.

32. See Barth, *Dogmatics* I/1, 88–124; Barth, "Significance of the Bible"; Barth, "Principle of Scripture."

can have no independent authority for liberal and progressive theologies. It can be affirmed as a valuable resource without which there would be no such thing as Christianity or the church (though we must always ask whether and to what extent Christianity and the church themselves have been and are good news and not bad news for the world). But if it is to be a life-giving resource, whatever the Bible can be said to *mean* for the church and for the world, whatever ways it can be used to form and inform, to guide and direct the Christian life and community, must be wholly under the interpretive authority of those communities who choose to risk continuing to engage it as Scripture, particularly those communities in relation to whom it has been used to marginalize, denigrate, exclude, and to otherwise do harm.

On the other hand, cutting against conservative theologies on the right, Barth's turn to the Bible is insufficient because it only acknowledges and affirms the *relative* authority of the Bible. As we have seen, in its function as the authoritative *human witness to* the Word of God—i.e., to God for us all in Jesus (through the Spirit), the last, first—the Bible is not *in itself* the Word of God, whether sitting over there on the table or held in one's hand or memorized in one's heart or heard from the mouth of the preacher. Only the living Trinitarian reality of God with and for us all in Jesus (through the Spirit), the last, first, as the concrete actualization of God's one eternal will and decision, is the Word of God *in itself*. Even when the Bible—e.g., the words of Paul—*becomes* the Word of God in a new, free event of divine speaking in and through the written words of human witness, its identity as the Word of God is wholly relative to and absolutely dependent upon the *living* Word of God that only God can speak and enact, and that only occurs as an *event* of revelatory divine self-giving the content of which is God for us in Jesus (through the Spirit), the last, first.

This is much *less* authority than conservative and traditional theologies want to give the Bible, especially within the Protestant traditions and denominations. This notion that the Bible is not the Word of God in itself but only *becomes* the Word of God if and when God wills in freedom to speak through it is, for conservatives, a classic sign of Barth's crossing the line into hopeless liberalism. Theological conservatives tend to view the Bible in and of itself as the Word of God. It is seen as the *written* Word of God, equal in content and authority to the *living* Word of God that is Jesus Christ. From this point of view, Barth can only be seen as too theologically liberal, undermining the true foundation of traditional Christian faith.

The Bible as Site for Competing Natural Theologies

The nature, status, and authority of the Bible continues to be a decisive, conflictual fork in the road between theological liberals and progressives, on one hand, and theological conservatives and traditionalists, on the other—particularly in the Protestant world. *And Barth disagrees with them all.* The nature and authority of the Bible, then, is a decisive issue in and through which Barth can be seen to cut both ways in relation to the spectrum of theological alternatives. As I said at the outset, he is seen as too conservative on the Bible by theological liberals and progressives, and too liberal on the Bible by theological conservatives. Alternatively, Barth sees both the liberal-progressive and conservative approaches to the Bible as albeit very different versions of the same thing; he sees them both as attempts to seize control of and appropriate the free and living Word of God as a human possession, possibility, and capacity. That is, for Barth, they are both forms of what he calls natural theology. Liberal-progressive theologies subjugate the biblical witness to a symbolically interpreted "Word of God" that is understood to be in continuity with, if not identical to, the human word of natural human religious experience, vision, and expression. Conservative theologies identify the Bible itself as the Word of God, putting the latter at our disposal, to be picked up and wielded by the human being, taken up into human hands, into the human heart and mouth, according to and so under the control of the human being's discretion, desire, whim, or need.

We need to see one more thing here, if we are really to catch sight of the way in which Barth cuts both ways on the theological spectrum. It is not that Barth feels conservative theology is too conservative and needs to be a little more liberal, and that liberal theology is too liberal and needs to be a little more conservative, so that they might meet at some Aristotelian balance-point somewhere in the middle, where Jesus lives. Barth does not have his eye on the theological (or the political) spectrum. For Barth, Jesus does not live on our theological (or political) spectrums, much less in the Aristotelian middle. Consequently, to be what is judged as appropriately "conservative" or appropriately "liberal" (or "orthodox" or "progressive" or "liberationist"), or appropriately neither, according to the cultural markers and criteria of whatever context we happen to be in, is not the point. For Barth, the point is to hear and respond to the Word of God that is God with and for us *all* in Jesus (through the Spirit), *the last, first,* as given witness by the biblical prophets and apostles, as faithfully and responsibly as one can. Wherever this hearing and responding places one on whatever theological (or political) spectrums happen to be in fashion and holding sway in whatever concrete historical context we happen to be in is, at most, a secondary matter. If we play to the prevailing winds of context, no matter how compelling we find them, Barth believes we will inevitably diminish the radical goodness of the news. In this light, Barth can be seen as more "radical," in the technical sense of the term, than either the conservative or the progressive, relativizing any and all spectrums upon which both parties stake their claims, and the zero-sum competitions through which the current contesting categories, locations, and identities receive their meaning. Barth's cutting both ways does not ensconce him—or at least the gospel to which he is attempting, often poorly, to point—snugly in the middle of the theological spectrum, but critically relativizes the spectrum itself.

Finally, then, for Barth, turning to the Bible does *not* guarantee either the *truth* or the *goodness* of the news about Jesus that the church is called to confess. It does *not* guarantee and secure our knowledge of or relation to God. It is true that, for Barth, there is no gospel for Christians and churches without the prophetic and apostolic witness in Scripture, and that Christians and churches cannot be what they are called to be without that witness. We cannot hear the good news that God is concretely, unqualifiedly, and irrevocably for us all in Jesus (through the Spirit), the last, first, nor a commission to proclaim and live out that good news in embodied word and deed, without the prophetic and apostolic witness within the Bible. However, while it does function as a corrective against what Barth sees as certain temptations of liberal theology, the Bible cannot provide any of conservative theology's desired security and control in relation to the truth and goodness of the gospel, much less in relation to the God of whose radical, redeeming self-giving and self-disclosure to and for the creature the gospel is believed to be a report. For Barth, Christians and churches can only understand themselves to be addressed, gathered, and commissioned by the biblical witness to the one eternal will, decision, Word, and act of God to be for and *only* for the sin-bound creature, the last, first, made concretely actual in Jesus (through the Spirit). But in holding the Bible in our hands, Christians and churches hold neither divine truth nor divine authority. For Barth, divine truth and divine authority reside neither in the Bible nor in churches nor in Christians, but only in the living God.

QUESTIONS

1. What does even Barth acknowledge as positive and compelling features of the liberal theology of the nineteenth century, especially as a critique

of and correction to older ecclesial and theological orthodoxies and their reactionary, closed resistance to the discoveries and developments of the modern world?

2. Can you think of any particular instances of what I identify parenthetically throughout the chapter as the problematic limit of liberal theology's vision in nineteenth-century Europe: its Eurocentric, colonialist, patriarchal, and classist assumptions? How are you and your faith community located in relation to these realities, and how have you been impacted by them, either by being marginalized or privileged by them? In what ways can the same things be said of traditional/conservative theologies in your experience?

3. How did the liberal theology of the nineteenth century, at least as Barth understood it, view (a) the divine-human relation, and (b) the grounds—the theological starting point—for our knowledge of that relation? What did Barth come to see as the primary problems of this view? How did the First World War and the movement of socialism demonstrate the problematic limits of liberal theology, for Barth?

4. How was Barth's "turn to the Bible" not a *re*-turn to the Bible? That is, how was it not a reaffirmation of the theologically conservative, Biblicist, and inerrantist claims about the nature and authority of Scripture that rejected the developments of liberal theology from the get-go?

5. How does Barth's view of Scripture as authoritative *human* witness to the Word of God for the church—that can *become* the Word of God *if and when* God wills and acts, by speaking through it—"cut both ways" in relation to theologically conservative approaches on the right and liberal-progressive approaches on the left? That is, how does it not affirm *enough* for the former and affirm *too much* for the latter? Where are you and your faith community located in this debate? Do you find Barth's view compelling or problematic? Why?

4

THE MOVEMENT OF BARTH'S THEOLOGICAL LOGIC

—from God

AS WE HAVE SEEN, Barth's early emphasis on the radical transcendence of God as strange and unknown "Wholly Other" was not a theological corrective he conjured up on the basis of his diagnosis of the failure of the liberal theology of the nineteenth century. As Barth tells it, at least, he discovered—or was encountered by, surprised by—an unknown God after turning to the Bible as a desperate "Hail Mary" in search of a new starting point for theology. The God he discovered in the Bible was a stranger and enemy to whatever presumed to be the highest human understanding, the best and brightest human projects. This vision of the otherness of God "took" in that context because, once discovered, it did indeed appear to be a pertinent theological corrective to the fundamental methodological commitments of liberal theology. If we did *not*, in fact, know and relate to God on the basis of our own presumedly sophisticated self-knowledge (whether rooted in reason or aesthetics/creativity or experience), grounded in our metaphysical or ontological constitution, then perhaps there was hope, given that liberal theology's assumption that we *did* know and relate to God in this way appeared to fail in the face of unprecedented catastrophe.

The alternative that presented itself to—or, as Barth would no doubt prefer to put it, impressed and imposed itself upon—Barth and Thurneysen in their turn to the Bible was that knowledge of God, together with all that is entailed in our relation to God, comes to us always only *from God*, that is, as an impossible possibility, from outside of and far beyond all natural, creaturely possibility. Which, of course, is simply another way of saying that the possibility and actuality of our knowledge of and relation to God does *not* come from—does not begin with nor is it grounded in—*ourselves*; is *not* a natural possibility and capacity of the creature. The affirmation and insistence, *from God*, then, is consistent with and central to both Barth's turn to a grounding for Christian theology that is different from that of liberal theology and his no to all forms of what he calls natural theology, whether liberal or conservative.

That said, I propose the theological affirmation and insistence entailed in the prepositional phrase *from God*, which Barth uses regularly and which I have already found it necessary to use at certain points, as a helpful interpretive key to the fundamental theological logic that governs the entirety of Barth's theology.[1] It also serves as a helpful interpretive lens for understanding his distinctive approach to key elements of the doctrine of God.

THE THEOLOGICAL LOGIC OF THE GOSPEL: THE IRREVERSIBLE ORDER AND PRIORITY OF THE GOD-HUMAN RELATION

The prepositional phrase *from God* can be taken as shorthand for the theological logic and order Barth believes is inherent in and necessary to the goodness of the gospel and so of all Christian thinking and speaking about the gospel. For Barth, the gospel is the news of God's redeeming and reconciling action on behalf of the creature, calling the creature into relation and so to response in creaturely freedom and responsibility. In every point of this story and in all its dimensions, God is the primary actor and the initiator of all the action, of all that transpires between God and the creature, of all possibility and actuality. At every point of the gospel and every dimension of faith in that gospel, it is always God who wills and acts first—indeed, from all eternity, from before the foundations of the world.[2]

---

1. See, for example: "knowledge of God from God . . ." (Barth, *Dogmatics* I/1, 119, 120); "It will just be true from God . . ." (Barth, *Dogmatics* I/1, 222); "The Christian imperative runs: Expect everything from God, and from God everything" (Barth, "Christian Ethics," 113). See also: "How to think theologically? 'From God'" (Schwöbel, "Theology," 19).

2. For Barth, *from God* marks a strictly irreversible sequence, one that is made and revealed concretely once for all in the person, event, and relation that is Jesus Christ (in the Spirit). See, for example: "*He* is the initiator, founder, preserver, and fulfiller of the covenant. *He* is the sovereign Lord of the amazing relationship in which He becomes and is not only different from man but also one with him. He is also the creator of him who is His partner . . . As the Son of God and not otherwise, Jesus Christ is the Son of Man. This sequence is irreversible" (Barth, "Humanity of God," 48). Barth also applies this logic

This theological logic and order sets some concrete limits to a theological understanding of human life and human faith. To begin with, as we have seen, everything the creature is and does only means what it means as a response to divine initiating action to and for the creature. The creature can never begin at the beginning because God has always already begun, has always already been on the move. All of our so-called beginnings are only secondary responses and reactions within a story that has begun without us and that ultimately belongs to and is determined by another, and which, therefore, we cannot control.[3] Consequently, the creature can have nothing on their own terms, not even themselves. They only *are*—they only have their lives and the world—as creatures called forth into and for the sake of a very particular relation with God and, in God, with and for each other. This is not a story that we—including Christians and churches; *especially* Christians and churches—get to determine or direct or approve. As Barth says regularly: "We are not asked . . ."[4] We do not get script approval. It is a story we find ourselves caught up in as creatures called to respond to particular, concrete divine action and address.

Consequently, we do not get the first or final word over the meaning of our life or our actions or desires or dreams or visions or theological methods or personal faith practices or work for justice. The initiating will and act of God sets very specific and concrete parameters for all of creaturely life; parameters—it is important to note—that simultaneously function as the ground for and the call to the exercise of our creaturely freedom and responsibility. God wills and acts, calls and pursues, and all of creaturely life and activity is framed and determined as response to that divine overture, be

---

of irreversible sequence, order, and priority to the movement from cross to resurrection, the irreversible movement from judgment to salvation. This is a recurring theme in his doctrine of election (*Dogmatics* II/2).

3. The way in which this movement, *from God*, robs the human being of any and every possibility of mastery and control, in relation to either God or neighbor, is similar in effect to the "displacement of the modern subject" that is a central theme in postmodern philosophies and theologies. This is a central reason why Barth is seen by some as resonating with certain dimensions of postmodern philosophy and theology (especially that of Jacques Derrida and Emmanuel Levinas). See Ward, *Language of Theology*; Lowe, *Theology and Difference*; Boesel, "Apophasis of Divine Freedom"; Boesel, *Risking Proclamation*.

4. See, for example: "This message is as new and foreign and superior to the Church as it is to all the people to whom the Church is supposed to proclaim it. The Church can only deliver it the way a postman delivers his mail; the Church is not asked . . . what it makes of the message. The less it makes of it and the less it leaves on it its own fingerprints . . . so much the better" (Barth, "Proclamation of Free Grace," 49).

that response positive or negative, willing or resistant, a creaturely yes or a creaturely no.

Because Barth believes this ordering to be the way things actually *happen*—God initiates, we respond, with both the possibility and the meaning of the latter being determined and circumscribed by the former—he believes this should determine the ordering of the church's theological thinking and knowing, speaking and doing.[5] Whatever particular part or theme of the gospel or of Christian doctrine or of the life of faith is under discussion, this irreversible order, sequence, and priority is the light in which it must be seen, *if* Christians and churches are to be faithful and obedient to the one divine Word and action that calls us into existence and commissions us to concrete word and action.

Who's Doing What?

This strict theological ordering of the God-creature relationship may seem obvious to theologically conservative Christians—though, as we will see, it is an ordering that conservative theologies invariably and covertly find ways of avoiding and reversing through conservative forms of natural theology. Alternatively, within liberal and progressive contexts, the strict ordering of Barth's theology constitutes an explicit *reversal* of the usual run of things. Liberal and progressive theologies have most often built upon the concept of religion invented by eighteenth- and nineteenth-century European (male, propertied) academics in their attempt to come up with a scientific account of all dimensions of human life. Religion—including the Christian religion— is seen as the anthropological phenomenon of the human creature's search for God (or the Ultimate, the Universal, the Ground of Being—enter your

---

5. Seen from a certain angle, this theological logic of *from God* is similar to that of Thomas Aquinas, the paradigm of classical natural theology. For Aquinas, using Aristotle, God is like the First Cause, and creatures are effects of that Cause, such that creatures receive their being *from God*. The key difference, at least from Barth's point of view, is that the ontological relation of God/cause to creature/effect is an ever-flowing *process* continually and readily available and accessible to the latter, such that the creature can ascend up the down escalator, so to speak, through a disciplined use of reason, to arrive at certain truths about God as their own natural capacity and at their own initiative. For Barth, this places God and knowledge of God at our disposal. *Contra* Aquinas, then, Barth's *from God* is strictly determined as a particular, concrete, contingent *event* of redemptive personal encounter, an event that only occurs in and as an act of divine freedom. So while the relation between God and creature moves in the same direction, and is just as actual, as in Aquinas, it is never at our disposal.

preferred general metaphysical category here) and/or quest for ultimate meaning.

For Barth, however, the gospel is not the story of human religious searching for and finding God, ultimately discovering that God to be ineffable mystery. Divine mystery is not discovered as the fruit of our labor, our search, and our journey. On the contrary, Barth understands the gospel to be the story of a God who searches for and finds *us*, and who will not stop until *all* are found (*really* all, this time, not just all white, straight, propertied men—indeed, *the last, first*).[6] It is *God's* concrete searching for and finding the creature that opens the story, that is the first chapter and the beginning of *every* chapter. It is decidedly not, then, the story of *our* discovery of God as ineffable mystery, recounted as the crowning achievement of our religious quest in the final chapter of *our* memoir.

Rather than us doing all the work in our questing for God and ultimate meaning, Barth would rather err in the other direction. Indeed, it often seems like, for Barth, it is God who seems to be doing all the work in searching for and finding us. In the relation between God and the creature, it is the will and work of *God* that sets the context and parameters for the work of the creature. The work of the latter, whatever that might be, must always be seen in this light—a rather disappointing light if one has high hopes for being the star of the show or at least in control of the storyline.

As I noted earlier, while this theological ordering of divine initiative and priority may seem familiar and unsurprising to many conservative Christians, conservative faith has its own wily ways of fulfilling its desire for mastery and control, as made evident in conservative resistance to Barth's work. Certain forms of pietism and evangelicalism are very effective in talking a lot about God's transcendence and sovereignty and divine initiative and

---

6. See, for example: "For we do not find the Word of God in the reality present to us. Rather—and this is something quite different—the Word of God *finds us* in the reality present to us. Again, it cannot be produced again out of our direct experience. Whenever we know it, we are rather begotten by it . . ." (Barth, *Dogmatics* I/1, 195–96; my emphasis); "He (the person of faith) has not created his own faith; the Word has created it. He has not come to faith; faith has come to him through the Word. He has not adopted faith; faith has been granted to him through the Word" (Barth, *Dogmatics* I/1, 244); "If we soar up into these heights . . . it simply means that we willfully hurry past God, who descends in His revelation into this world of ours. Instead of finding Him where He Himself has sought us . . . we seek Him where He is not to be found, since He on His side seeks us in His Word" (Barth, *Dogmatics* II/1, 11); "Knowledge of revelation . . . is a concrete knowledge of the God who has sought man and meets him in his concrete situation . . . there indeed it becomes manifest also that man belongs to God not because he is capable of God, not because he has sought and found him, but because it is God's gracious will to make man His own" (Barth, "Revelation," 11–12).

priority, all the while placing control over the eternal meaning and destiny of the individual human being thoroughly within their own hands. For example, in many forms of pietism and evangelicalism, it is *my* faith in God, *my* act of accepting God's provision for sin in Jesus, *my* decision to accept God's offer of forgiveness by accepting Jesus into my heart as my personal Lord and Savior, etc., that ultimately determines the eternal meaning and destiny of my creaturely life. God provides provision, but I am ultimately in control of what that means for my life, of whether that provision is made effective for me or not. I determine the storyline. I star in the critical scene upon which everything—nothing less than my eternal destiny—depends. Much to the chagrin of many conservative theologies, Barth disappropriates the human creature of any such final script approval and control over their own storyline, as well as over the role of God in that storyline.

Again, in relation to both progressive and conservative desires to be in control of our story and so of God's story—albeit in order to ensure the goodness of the gospel—Barth believes, whether wrongly or rightly, foolishly or wisely, that it is only when *God* is the primary actor in a story primarily about God and only secondarily about us, as the sought-after beloved of God, that the gospel news can be truly good for anyone, be it ourselves, the neighbor, or all of creation. More accurately, Barth believes we can only be truly assured that this is the case when we are speaking about the God who gives Godself wholly, fully, and concretely to the creature to be known and loved in Jesus (through the Spirit), the last, first. A pivotal signpost: Barth believes that God—*this particular God, in this particular, concrete, unequivocal, and irrevocable self-giving*—is better for us and our neighbor than we are able to be for ourselves and for our neighbors. My neighbor and I are better off in God's hands, come what may, than we are in my hands.

Finally, then, we come to an important question that must always be asked of theological interpretation of the gospel when one is thinking with Barth: *Who's doing what?* What is God doing? What are we doing? And how are these doings related?

As concerns the question about what *God* does or is doing: *from God* helps us see the distinctive way in which Barth approaches and understands several key dimensions of traditional doctrines of God. This is especially important because of the extent to which certain inherited conceptions of these classic themes are familiar to many Christians and carry so much weight in terms of the church's often unexamined habits of theological thinking. We think we know what these doctrinal terms mean. However, while Barth uses much of the traditional theological language in his understanding of God, that language does not necessarily mean what we think it means when Barth is using it. He often defines and deploys this language in ways that move against the grain of the church's traditional thinking. This is because, for Barth, these themes and doctrinal terms can only mean what they mean as informed and determined by the one eternal Word of God that is God for us all in Jesus (through the Spirit), the last, first; that is, the one Word of God that has come and always comes to us *from God*.

DIVINE TRANSCENDENCE AS MODE OF DIVINE IMMANENCE: GOD WITH, FOR, AND AS THE CREATURE

As has already been mentioned, if the reader has heard anything about Barth, it is probably that he rediscovered and reasserted God's radical transcendence in and for Christian theology, describing God as the Wholly Other. While the wholly otherness of God was certainly a critical component of Barth's early theology, and perhaps the single issue most responsible for the theological revolution it ignited early in the twentieth century, it is a mischaracterization of Barth's theology to say that God as the Wholly Other was—and remained—the central issue of his theology or even, more specifically, of his understanding of God.

As we have already seen, albeit briefly, Barth's version of divine transcendence is not primarily about God's absolute difference and distance from us. Where's the good news in that? Yes, it functions negatively as a critical leverage against idolatry, and that is important. But it does not tell us anything concretely positive about God's decisive intention and action in relation to the creature and creation. After all, the divine transcendence that Barth discovered in the prophetic and apostolic witness within the Bible is the transcendence of a God who nevertheless creates an "other" for the sake of a covenant relation, and who relentlessly pursues that other and that relation in the face of every obstacle and every failure and betrayal—even in the face of the ultimate enemy, sin and death—stubbornly refusing to give up on that other and that relation. The point of recognizing the particular reality of God's transcendence, for Barth—of getting it "right" (as best we can, in frail, questionable, and always sinful human understanding and witness)—is to properly acknowledge and recognize the particular, concrete *way* of God's radical and irrevocable *intimacy with* us, the intimacy in, with, and for which God seeks and finds us, the particular *way* and *how* of the gospel's "God with us."

Most importantly for Barth, the particular mode of God's immanence——i.e., of the irrevocable intimacy of the gospel's "God with us"—is not simply or even primarily metaphysical or ontological. God is also—and primarily—intentionally and so personally with and for creation and the creature. God is distinctively present to and with creation and the creature—concretely in the living, personal reality and history of Jesus (through the Spirit)—as the result of a divine decision for a very *particular kind* of relation above and beyond the necessity entailed in merely metaphysical or ontological relation.

The key point for Barth, then, is not to affirm and assert divine transcendence for its own sake, but only as it serves the goodness of the gospel news that God is with and for us in and for a *particular kind* of relation: the fellowship and communion of covenant partners free for each other in love and responsibility. For Barth, divine transcendence characterizes the particular mode of God's *immanence* in, with, and for creation. Divine transcendence does not mean there is no knowledge of or intimate relation with God. It means that the intimate knowledge of and relation to God that does, in fact, occur is always only *from God*, in an event of free divine self-giving, and not a naturally available possession at our disposal via our metaphysical or ontological constitution. But in this way—*from God* in free divine self-giving—God *really does come to us*, in the most concrete and intimate way. Barth's understanding of divine transcendence not only resists the ever-present temptations of idolatry—the remaking of God into a possession we control—but also marks the very particular way in which God really does give Godself to us wholly and unqualifiedly and irrevocably: in and through free personal intention and decision, above and beyond metaphysical and ontological necessity, to be known and loved in responsible freedom, to and for personal relations of fellowship and communion—the creature with God, and in God, with and for each other, the last, first. And, Barth assumes, this is cause for great rejoicing.

DIVINE SOVEREIGNTY: A LIMIT ON DESTRUCTIVE POWERS

As we have seen, the initiating divine will, decision, Word, and action in which all creaturely knowledge of and relation to God is rooted sets concrete parameters for the creaturely sphere. Within this creaturely sphere, every dimension of our creaturely life can only be response to specific, concrete divine action and address. We are thereby always already dispossessed of any final ultimate control over the context and meaning of our, or our neighbor's, life. This is a helpful way to think about Barth's version of divine sovereignty.

Barth's theology is primarily located in and informed by the Reformed tradition, with its roots in Calvin. Not surprisingly, then, divine sovereignty is a key theme in his theology. However, Barth critiques and departs from what most people *think of* as TULIP Calvinism's version of sovereignty in important ways.

For Barth, divine sovereignty is not a form of power and control that infringes upon or severely limits creaturely power, agency, freedom, or responsibility, as if God were a cosmic puppet master and we were mere puppets, mere automatons going through the motions of fulfilling the divine will at every moment. (Nor is this true of Calvin's view of divine sovereignty, though it is often caricatured in this way.) God does not compete with creatures for power and control, as if more divine power and control means less power and control for the creature. This is to misunderstand the true nature of divine transcendence. As Kathryn Tanner has pointed out, this view reduces divine transcendence to the terms of immanence, pulling it within the sphere of our comprehension and categories as something that we can size up, compare, and take the measure of, as another thing alongside of and commensurable with everything that is within—i.e., immanent to—the sphere of our experience and knowledge.[7] By contrast, when radical transcendence is kept in view, it involves a radically non-competitive relation, such that God's power and control can be seen as the *ground and source* of creaturely power and agency, not its infringement or negation, even as it marks the latter's ultimate parameters.

Neither does divine sovereignty sanctify and justify human claims to sovereignty and the creaturely exercise of power and control in God's name (e.g., as in the history of political monarchies). This is again to reduce the category of divine transcendence to the terms of immanence, putting divine power in continuity with creaturely power, a power to be wielded by some creatures over others. The radical transcendence of genuine divine sovereignty undermines, overturns, and stands in judgment over-against all creaturely claims to sovereignty, especially claims to divinely ordained sovereignty, and its exercise of power and control. A banner headline for understanding Barth on sovereignty: if *God* is sovereign, *no one else is, can, or should be!* And if by God we mean the *particular* God who is eternally and concretely for us in the material, historical vulnerability of Jesus (in and through the Spirit), the last, first, then the sovereignty of *this* God can never be a theological justification for creaturely sovereignty as destructive control and power over others, as, for example, the creaturely sovereignty desired and claimed by empire.

---

7. See Tanner, *God and Creation*, 152.

Consequently, Barth's view of divine sovereignty is not so much about power and control, especially as those terms are defined by our historical experience in a sinful and broken world. It has more to do with scope and parental care. For Barth, divine sovereignty primarily means that nothing exists or occurs—in heaven, on earth, or in hell—that is beyond or absolutely outside of and so fundamentally and effectively obstructive in relation to God's eternal will and intention to be redemptively with and for us in Jesus (through the Spirit).

Yes, the divine sovereignty suggested by the theological logic of *from God* does set the parameters of the creaturely sphere and so of the ultimate meaning of all creaturely power, agency, freedom, and responsibility, even while it functions as the ground of all creaturely power, agency, freedom, and responsibility within those parameters. However, these parameters are not an arbitrary set of lines or boundaries set by God, designed to box the creature in, to keep the creature at a safe distance and under control. Rather, the parameters of creaturely existence are nothing but God's very self and self-giving to and for the creature; God's eternal yet concrete will, intention, and action for the sake of a particular kind of relation with the creature; God's initiating movement toward and pursuit of the creature.

For Barth, then, divine sovereignty, as understood through the lens of *from God* means that nothing and no one—not Satan, not the powers and principalities, not the idols of this world (e.g., racism, sexism, homophobia, ableism, greed, free market forces, nationalism, militarism, to name a few), and not even ourselves—can ultimately obstruct, foil, or prevent God's will and intention to be with, for, and as the creature irrevocably and unqualifiedly in the one divine Word and act that is God for us in Jesus (through the Spirit), the last, first. Every creature and all of creation—from eternity to eternity and in the midst of history, indeed, in and from the underside of history—are always in the caring, loving hands of God whose eternal will and intention for us is the peace and mutual blessing of fellowship and communion with God and neighbor. Nothing—not even ourselves—can tear us away or snatch us from those hands or that eternal will and intention of parental care.

For Barth, then, divine sovereignty is clearly a *good* thing. It is theologically important—yea, vital—because it functions to assure the goodness of the news that, because *God is for us* in a very concrete and particular way, nothing can finally or successfully be against us. It assures us that—at every moment, in every place, even in the midst of hell—we are in God's good hands and so cannot ultimately be destroyed, nor can we destroy ourselves or our neighbor. Only God can destroy us, and God—as our one and only true judge—has from all eternity willed to be and has concretely become not only our creator and judge but our savior, partner, and friend. *Therefore!* as Paul might say, *this* sovereignty, of *this* God, means there is no limit to the goodness of the news in Barth's theological vision. Because God is eternally for us all in Jesus (through the Spirit), for all creatures and all creation, the last, first, nothing can finally stand against us or destroy us or finally obstruct or separate us from that eternal will in its concrete actuality.[8]

DIVINE SOVEREIGNTY AND DIVINE FREEDOM

Another key to understanding Barth's take on divine sovereignty is to recognize its essential link to divine freedom. Indeed, it might be more accurate to say that Barth's understanding of and commitment to divine freedom determines his view of sovereignty rather than vice versa. After all, the working short-hand for his doctrine of God is "the God who loves in freedom," not "the God who loves in sovereignty." There are several reasons why divine *freedom* is so important to Barth's doctrine of God, even more so than sovereignty or omnipotence or any of the "omnis," or any of the other non-personal attributes generally ascribed to God in a traditional Christian doctrine of God. We have already caught a glimpse of these reasons when looking at Barth's view of transcendence and sovereignty.

Divine Freedom and Divine Love

The radical freedom of God's willing, intending, and acting is important for Barth because it witnesses to the nature of God's self-giving to the creature in Jesus (through the Spirit), the last, first, as wholly an act of love. The theological logic of *from God* means God's will, decision, Word, and act to be with and

---

8. See, for example: "The Subject of election . . . is not in the least a 'God in general,' as he may be conceived and systematically constructed from the standpoint of sovereignty, or omnipotence, of a first cause, of absolute necessity . . . the true God is the One whose freedom and love have nothing to do with abstract absoluteness or naked sovereignty, but who in His love and freedom has determined and limited Himself to be God in particular and not in general, and only as such to be omnipotent and sovereign . . . The true God . . . is, of course, the sovereign Lord and Ruler of all things and all events . . . [but] in this name [Jesus Christ] . . . we discern the divine decision in favour of the movement towards this people, and the self-determination of God as Lord and Shepherd of this people, and the determination of this people as 'his people, and the sheep of his pasture' . . . under this name . . . God Himself . . . directs upon it [this people] a love no less than that with which in the person of the Son He loves Himself . . ." (Barth, *Dogmatics* II/2, 49ff). See also in *Dogmatics* II/2, "The Eternal Will of God in the Election of Jesus Christ," 145–94.

for the creature, the last, first, is rooted solely and moves wholly out of God's self and so out of God's freedom. It is not driven by any external or internal metaphysical necessity. It is not subject to any external or internal force or principle. It is not a function of God's metaphysical constitution or the metaphysical constitution of reality in general. For Barth, God does not *have to* or *need to* create the creature and creation for concrete relation, or give Godself to the creature and creation for the sake of that relation. God *chooses* to create and be concretely with, for, and as the creature in freedom, as an act of utter gratuity. This is Barth's understanding of God's love: being radically for the creature wholly free of necessity, compulsion, coercion, force, or principle— simply for the sake of the creature and so for love of the creature.[9]

It is important to note here that the radical nature of divine freedom, for Barth, does not mean that it is a radically *arbitrary* kind of freedom, as if a mere whim, rooted in nothing, entirely cut off from any context or anything essential to God's nature. The radical freedom of God's decision to be with and for the creature means it is solely an expression of who God is in God's self, an expression of and outpouring of God's eternal Trinitarian life of loving freedom. For Barth, God *is* the God who loves in freedom. The Trinitarian persons are who they are as persons free for each other in love.[10] Barth's Trinitarian God is the God who from eternity to eternity loves in freedom. To be addressed, encountered, and pursued by *this* God, *from God*, means being sought and found by the God whose very nature is to be free for the other in love. God's being with, for, and as the creature in loving freedom is nothing but the outpouring of God's essential nature. The fact that all things, especially *God*, come to us *from God*—from this *particular* God—means that the foundation of the parameters, content, and meaning of creaturely existence itself is the divine call into, and actualization of, concrete freedom for the other in love.

---

9. See "The Being of God as the One who Loves," in Barth, *Dogmatics* II/1, 272–97. See, for example: "God is He who, without having to do so, seeks and creates fellowship between Himself and us. He does not have to do it . . . It implies so to speak an overflow of His essence that He turns to us . . . it is an overflow which is not demanded or presupposed by any necessity, constraint, or obligation, least of all from outside, from our side, or by any law by which God Himself is bound and obliged. On the contrary . . . it is again rooted in Himself alone" (Barth, *Dogmatics* II/1, 273).

10. See "The Being of God as the One Who Loves in Freedom," in Barth, *Dogmatics* II/1, 257–321. See, for example: "God is who He is in the act of His revelation. God seeks and creates fellowship between Himself and us, and therefore He loves us. But He is this loving God without us, as Father, Son and Holy Spirit, in the freedom of the Lord, who has His life from Himself" (Barth, *Dogmatics* II/1, 257).

So again, the unqualified goodness of the news for Barth: God's very self, and so all of existence, and so every dimension of God's relation with created reality and with the human creature—including divine wrath over and judgment of sin's destructive hold upon the creature and creation—are expressions of God's eternal, freely given love for the creature and creation; of God's desire for a particular kind of relation, a concrete relation of love in responsible freedom with the creature amidst creation; and of God's commitment to actualize and ensure that relation for the sake of every creature and of all creation, the last, first.

Divine Freedom and Divine Mystery

For Barth, divine freedom means God is free from any and all external compulsion or control upon or over God's will, decision, and action. This is important for Barth because, as we have seen, for Barth, God's one eternal will, decision, and action is to be God *only with, for, and as the creature*. It is good news, therefore, that this will, decision, and action is ultimately free from any outside interference, coercion, or obstruction, including any and all interference or obstruction from creatures themselves.

This corresponds to what we have already seen of Barth's allergy to all the ways in which the human creature, *especially the religious and theological human creature*, is always attempting to bring divine reality—i.e., the free and loving Word and action of God—under human control, under the authority of human sanction and approval. And I have shown how this issue is at the heart of his no to all forms of natural theology. There is no theological method, concept, or starting point that places God in our hands as a natural capacity and possession and thereby places God at our disposal, and any method, concept, or starting point that attempts to do so can only be distorting and destructive. This divine freedom from creaturely mastery and control, especially in relation to the possibilities and capacities of human reason, thought, conceptuality, and expectation means that, for Barth, Christian faith and all its theological work is always engaged by and a response to what is ultimately, first and last, divine mystery.[11]

11. See, for example, "The Speech of God as the Mystery of God," in Barth, *Dogmatics* I/1, 162–86. See especially: "The issue [the Word of God as the mystery of God] is not an ultimate 'assuring' but always a penultimate 'de-assuring' of theology, or, as one might put it, a theological warning against theology, a warning against the idea that its propositions or principles are certain in themselves like the supposed axioms of the mathematicians and physicists, and are not rather related to their theme and content, which alone are certain, which they cannot master, by which they must be mastered if they are not to be mere soap-bubbles" (Barth, *Dogmatics* I/1, 164–65).

The way divine freedom is related to divine mystery, for Barth, marks another difference between his theology and both the liberal and progressive alternatives on the left and the conservative options on the right. Liberal and progressive theologies have their own very compelling way of appealing to divine mystery in order to prevent God from becoming grasped as our possession, as at our disposal and so under our mastery and control. This approach has much in common with the ancient apophatic tradition of negative theology, which prioritizes the essential ineffability and incomprehensibility and so ultimate unknowability of the divine essence.[12] For Barth, this would be a perfectly legitimate move for Christian theology except for one tiny complication: the gospel. An apophatic version of divine transcendence runs into an extremely annoying and embarrassing limit when encountered by the prophetic and apostolic news that the radically unknowable God has, in fact, given Godself just as radically to the creature in an irrevocably concrete act of self-giving and self-disclosure precisely *to be known* (indeed, to be touched and held; a material vulnerability that does not escape torture and execution by the state) for the sake of a concrete covenant relation of love and responsibility.[13]

The reader should at this point be able to appreciate the irony that, on one hand, Barth is famous for emphasizing the radical transcendence of God as Wholly Other and therefore as *wholly unknowable* according to any natural creaturely capacity or possibility, while on the other hand, being equally well

12. The tradition of negative theology—or the *via negativa* (the way of negation)—is a strand of ancient theology stressing the ultimate mystery of God such that God's nature and essence are radically beyond all creaturely knowing and speaking. It teaches that we can only speak *truly* of God by saying what God is *not*, or by *unsaying* everything that we do in fact say theologically about God as creatures. This practice of *unsaying* is to speak *apophatically*, and it is to always accompany and supersede *cataphatic* speech (speech with positive content) about God. Influential theologians in this tradition include Pseudo-Dionysius, Nicolas of Cusa, and Meister Eckhart. There is currently a resurgence of apophatic approaches to theology in the wake of progressive theological engagement with postmodern philosophies, particularly that of Jacques Derrida. See John Caputo's recent work, beginning with Caputo, *Weakness of God*; see also, Keller, *Cloud of the Impossible*; Boesel and Keller, *Apophatic Bodies*. For a Barthian/Kierkegaardian response, see Boesel, *In Kierkegaard's Garden*.

13. See, for example: "Mystery does not just denote the hiddenness of God but His *revelation* in a hidden, i.e., a non-apparent way which intimates indirectly rather than directly. Mystery is the concealment of God *in which He meets us precisely when He unveils Himself to us* . . . Mystery thus denotes the *divine givenness* of the Word of God which also fixes our own limits and by which it distinguishes itself from everything that is given otherwise . . . This means that we cannot establish its distinction . . . Its distinguishes itself . . . not in such a way that we can arrive at a triumphant distinction, but in such a way that there is reserved for it the right to distinguish itself" (Barth, *Dogmatics* I/1, 165).

known as a theologian of *revelation*—i.e., a theologian emphasizing God's act of self-revelation as the ground of *actual creaturely knowledge of God*. Again, if one can understand the dialectical theological logic by which both are true of Barth without getting lost in mere logical contradiction, then one is well on the way to understanding the gist of his theology. For Barth, the unknown God gives Godself to be fully known by the creature in Jesus (through the Spirit), both in the concrete, living, personal reality that is the historical and resurrected Jesus as God incarnate, and through the always fragile, questionable, and, yes, sinful creaturely witness to that reality, that is, through Scripture and church proclamation *if and when God chooses to speak and act through them* (and also, *if God so wills*—lest the church ever overestimate its own importance [which, let's face it, it always does]—"through Russian Communism, a flute concerto, a blossoming shrub, or a dead dog").[14]

Consequently, to the extent that, for Barth, the gospel proclaims a very specific knowledge of God in God's concrete divine self-giving, then *privileging* the apophatic appeal to the essential unknowability of God as our primary theological responsibility is simply not an option for Christian theology and faith. This is related to what I would argue is the other side of progressive mischaracterizations of Barth's theology (the first side being that he is primarily a theologian of radical transcendence, of the unknown God): liberal and progressive theologies tend to interpret Barth's emphasis on God's self-revelation uniquely and concretely in Jesus (through the Spirit) and the biblical witness (again, through the Spirit) as violating divine mystery and placing it within the grasp of our knowledge and so our control. However, Barth contends that this can never be the case because of the radical divine freedom in and with which this revelatory divine self-giving and self-disclosure occurs.

For Barth, God's giving Godself to be known in and for love always occurs in and as a living free *event* of divine self-giving and self-disclosure, an event that the creature cannot anticipate, conjure, or create, nor take into their possession to determine, limit, or control. And the divine freedom of this event performs its own apophatic-like gesture.[15] It witnesses to the impossibility of creaturely control over and possession of God even as it witnesses

---

14. Barth, *Dogmatics* I/1, 55. See, for example: God's Word "is present and at work *when and where it wills* to be present and to be at work" (Barth, *Dogmatics* I/1, 90); "We have it [the Word of God] as it gives itself to us *if* we have it" (Barth, *Dogmatics* I/1, 91); "To bring it about that the *Deus dixit* [God speaks!] is present with the Church in its various times and situations is not in the power of the Bible or proclamation. The *Deus dixit* is true . . . *where and when* God . . . wills . . . that it be true, *where and when* God . . . lets it become true" (Barth, *Dogmatics* I/1, 120; all emphases are mine).

15. See Boesel, "Apophasis of Divine Freedom."

to the actuality of the knowledge of God that occurs in the event of God's free self-giving and self-disclosure to the creature to be known and loved in creaturely responsibility and freedom. As Barth often puts it, God is and remains *Lord* over the history of the God-human encounter and relation, Lord over the event in which the Word of God is spoken and heard, yet never *possessed* in human mastery or control.

Now, it must be noted that Barth's frequent and untroubled use of Lord and Lordship in reference to God is troubling for liberal- and progressive-minded Christians. Lordship implies power, and progressive and liberation theologies have helped us see how power in the creaturely realm most often boils down to destructive *power over*. Given this history and experience of destructive creaturely power in the form of creaturely lords and lordships, progressive and many liberationist theological convictions tend to see the traditional theological application of Lordship to God as simply (a) investing God with absolutely uncontestable destructive *power over*, which then (b) can be used to justify creaturely *power over*, as when the emperor and/or the empire claims to be God's representative power on earth, or when white people claim divinely ordained power over peoples of color. If this is the only way that the theological concept of divine Lordship works, then this is truly a recipe for a toxic doctrine of God and must be rejected. Barth, however, as we have already been seeing, is not convinced that this is the only way divine Lordship works—at least not when we are speaking of the *particular* divinity known concretely in Jesus (through the Spirit). Put differently, he sees that, *according to progressive theological assumptions*, this is indeed the only way that divine Lordship can be understood to work. But for Barth, liberal and progressive theological assumptions do not exhaust our theological options; they are just as historically determined, contingent, and contestable as everything else.

For Barth, then—given his primary theological assumption that the theological logic of the gospel moves *from God* to us and not *from us* to God; an explicit reversal of the movement of liberal theology—divine Lordship, like Barth's view of divine sovereignty and omnipotence, is not naked and abstract divine *power over*. Rather, it is always and only determined and limited by God's eternal decision to be God *only with and for and as* the creature and creation in the vulnerability of Jesus (in the Spirit) for the sake of fellowship and communion in love and justice. Consequently, divine Lordship, for Barth, is primarily divine *power for*—specifically, *for the redemptive well-being, wholeness, mutuality, and flourishing of the creature*, of *all* creatures, and of *all* creation, *the last, first*. In this very particular way, to the extent that divine Lordship is also a very particular and qualified form of *power over*, it is power over *all maleficent powers and forces*—that is, *all creaturely lords and lordships*—both on earth and in heaven, material and spiritual, that would oppose and obstruct this divine will for the creature and creation, that would seek the destruction of the creature and creation. (This brings us back to what is affirmed and what is rejected in Barth's understanding of divine sovereignty in terms of scope and parental care.) Seen in the light of the theological logic of the gospel, as Barth understands it, the Lordship of *this particular* God constitutes the radical rejection and judgment of all creaturely lords and lordships, especially when they are projected upon God and used to justify destructive creaturely *power over*.

If properly understood, then, Barth's view of revelation as an unanticipatable and unprovocable *event* of God's free yet concrete self-giving and self-disclosure in Jesus Christ (through the Spirit) does not necessarily violate divine mystery. Furthermore, it avoids what he would see as a concept of divine mystery inappropriate to the gospel news—i.e., a mystery wherein we really can't and don't know anything concrete about God—by faithfully responding to the distinctive mystery actually involved in the gospel: a strange and unknown God freely choosing to give Godself to the creature to be known and loved. The divine self-giving and self-disclosure, and the creaturely knowledge of God that occurs in the event of that self-giving and self-disclosure, remain essentially a mystery to us. They are from first to last beyond us, beyond our creaturely capacity or possibility. But—and this is critical for Barth's view of divine mystery—they are and remain beyond us *precisely in and by the very way that they do indeed come to us, that they are, in fact, given to us and made possible and actual for us.* The mystery isn't that we can't know God, it is *that* and *how* we *do* come to know the strange and unknowable God the way we do—actually and concretely, but never as our possibility or possession or as passing over into our control.

Finally, the connection between divine freedom and divine mystery in Barth allows us to see again the way in which Barth is always trying to do two different things in everything he does, to say two seemingly contradictory things at the same time in order to properly and faithfully—that is, dialectically—say the *one* thing he believes the church is called to say. *On one hand,* Barth is always trying to make it clear that and how God does what God does *as God*, i.e., in the mystery of divine freedom that always exceeds human capacity and control. While Barth believes liberal and progressive theologies have their ways of covertly gaining control over God's story and the God-relation precisely by emphasizing the mystery of divine unknowability, the most visible critical target of this move is the conservative tendency to claim to know God and speak of and for God—to know, possess, and speak the Word of God—even while affirming the miraculous source and nature of this knowledge.

On the other hand, Barth is always trying to make clear that, *as God*, God actually does some very concrete and particular things. That is, what God does, *as God*—i.e., in the mystery of divine freedom—is to give Godself wholly, unqualifiedly, irrevocably, and irreversibly *to and for the creature* to be known and loved in creaturely freedom and responsibility. While the unqualified and irreversible nature of this divine self-giving cuts against the grain of most conservative theology's need to limit the grace of God's self-giving (e.g., *someone* has to be burning in hell at the end of the story), the most visible and immediate critical target of this move is the liberal and progressive allergy to the possibility of real creaturely knowledge of God in and through a miraculous event of concrete, particular divine self-giving.

Divine Freedom and Radical Grace: *Sola Gratia*

Any discussion of Barth's view of divine freedom as the way in which God comes to us and is with and for us must include its essential relation to divine grace. Barth is in step with much historical Christian theological tradition in seeing divine freedom as the heart and soul of the distinctively theological concept of grace. Traditionally, grace names that which is given to us by God as free gift.[16] It names divine will, decision, and action as wholly unsolicited and unmerited, as entirely gratuitous divine initiative and decision *to and for the sake of the creature.*

For most historical theological traditions, the significance of grace as free gift is most often related to the theme of salvation: salvation as a free gift from God. While this is clearly affirmed by Augustine, and continues to be affirmed in qualified form in the Roman Catholic tradition, the idea of salvation by grace *alone* became a rallying cry for various Protestant reformations and continues to inform most Protestant traditions. Salvation from sin is seen as wholly undeserved and unmerited, and so a wholly free gift from God out of God's wholly gratuitous love, mercy, and forgiveness.

---

16. This theological definition of divine grace was hammered out rather distinctively by Augustine in his contest with the Pelagians. See Augustine, *Answer to the Pelagians*. The radical dimensions and implications of grace as truly *free*—sans Augustine's inescapable conclusion that unbaptized babies get sent to hell—were picked up again by Luther and Calvin and others in the Reformation movements of the sixteenth century.

This is key to the distinctive Protestant take on the goodness of the gospel news. We are freed from the hopeless attempt of having to earn our salvation through our own effort, our good works, our human righteousness. Because God works and gives salvation for and to us as a free gift, we in turn are freed from fear, despair, and the reign of death in our lives. The freedom of God's grace grounds and makes possible the human freedom to exercise our creaturely agency in gratitude and joy, free from the chains of fear and necessity. For most Protestant traditions, and for Barth, human cooperation with God's grace—to the extent that it is possible and actual—is not required for salvation itself (at least in principle), as in the Roman Catholic tradition. It is wholly a *consequence* of our salvation. We are freed by God's gracious gift of salvation to respond in creaturely freedom to and for both God and our neighbor in love and responsibility.[17]

While this is all true for Barth, the scope of divine freedom in his theology is much wider than the theme of salvation. Again, divine freedom is at the heart of God's eternal nature and being, as the Trinitarian God who loves in freedom. In determining God's own eternal life as Trinitarian relation of loving freedom, divine freedom determines every will, intention, and act of God, both in relation to God's self and in relation to all that is not God. Everything God does is decisively determined by and so done in and as an act of divine freedom. This means that everything that God does in relation to creation is decisively determined as an act of grace, in whole and in part, from first to last. God's eternally willed and historically concrete movement toward and for the creature is entirely determined as an act of grace. This includes the act of creation itself. The very creation of the creature, together with creation as a whole, is a gift of grace—an expression of God's loving freedom.[18] Given

---

17. Barth's thinking, here, while consistent with the Reformed view of the free gift of grace as making a claim upon the whole of our lives, can also be seen to resonate with Luther's view of Christian grace as freeing the Christian to do good works as God wills them to be done, in gratitude and joy, free from fear and necessity. See Luther, *Freedom of the Christian*.

18. See, for example: "In virtue of this self-determination of His [i.e., 'to be God only in this way,' as God *for* the creature in Jesus Christ], God is from the very first the gracious God. For this self-determination is identical with the decree of His movement towards man. This movement is always the very best thing that could happen to man" (Barth, *Dogmatics* II/2, 91–92); "For except with grace, and through grace, and to the glory of grace, there can be no rejoicing and praise of creation, no receiving of the Holy Spirit . . . Church doctrine must speak not only of God Himself, but also of all His ways and works . . . It must never speak as though it had to do with someone other than the gracious God. It must always give glory to God and bear witness to God as the gracious God . . . This doctrine [of election] is the basic witness to the fact that the gracious God is the beginning of all the ways and works of God. It defines grace as the starting-point for all reflection and utterance . . ." (Barth, *Dogmatics* II/2, 93).

that the free, initiating decision and action of God to and for the creature sets the parameters of creation and the creaturely sphere, this entire sphere is the sphere of grace, the sphere of God's free self-giving. Nothing exists outside or escapes from this sphere of God's grace.[19]

Cutting Both Ways: Not So Much Grace, Please

For Barth, one of the clearest and most consistent ways conservative theologies perform a version of natural theology's inevitable attempt to control God—and the neighbor, and creation—is in limiting the grace of God and thereby the goodness of the gospel news. As I've already noted, in virtually all of its historical forms, traditional Christian faith and theology has maintained an enduring and unswerving commitment to the vision that all must *not* be saved. Hell must be amply populated throughout eternity or the gospel has no meaning, from the traditional point of view. There's no point in being a Christian if someone—indeed, a good many people—is or are not burning in hell at the end of the story. (If you don't believe me, tell a conservative evangelical that *all* will be saved in the end and note the first thing that they say: But then, why should anyone believe? What would be the point of becoming a Christian? Trust me, this will happen *every* time.)

Conservative theologies traditionally ground this commitment to an eternally populated hell in the seemingly clear biblical witness to the fact that God is not only gracious, merciful, and forgiving, but also a holy and righteous judge.[20] We have caught glimpses of Barth's typically double-edged response to tradition on just this point, a response of both affirmation and critical correction. Affirmation: Barth agrees that this is indeed the biblical witness to who God is, and that Christian theology and faith must confess both God's merciful forgiveness of sinners and God's righteous judgment of sin. Critical correction: in seeing both God's merciful forgiveness and righteous judgment as rooted in and determined by the *one* divine will, decision,

---

19. For an important critical study of the centrality of grace in Barth's theology, see Berkouwer, *Triumph of Grace.*

20. Barth does not necessarily deny the reality of hell, he simply says that the church of Jesus Christ (in the Spirit) can never hope or believe that hell will be *eternally* populated. See, for example: "It is just the elect who, in view of their own election and in view of the rejected One who has taken all their sins to Himself [Jesus Christ], have no option but to expect of others too that this distinction may also become theirs, no matter who they are or wish to be . . . it would be to ignore Jesus Christ if we were to deny to others the hope upon which the elect themselves are also exclusively dependent—and even more, if we were not prepared to regard them wholly in the light of this hope" (Barth, *Dogmatics* II/2, 349–50).

Word, and act to be wholly, unequivocally, irrevocably, and irreversibly *with and for* the creature—yea, even and especially the *sinful* creature—in Jesus (through the Spirit), the last, first, Barth understands God's judgment of sin to be of a piece with God's salvation of the sinner.[21] He critiques tradition for separating its thinking about God from what it knows in Jesus Christ (through the Spirit). This enables it to separate God's gracious mercy from God's righteous judgment as two separate eternal wills in the life of God, with two separate ends: eternal life (for some) and eternal death (for most). As we have seen from the beginning, and will explore more in depth in the next chapter, when the church thinks about God before and apart from its confession about God being for us in Jesus (through the Spirit), the last, first, the gospel can only be a "mixed message of joy and terror," good news for some, bad news for most.

Further, in light of Barth's critique, the often unstated commitment of traditional conservative theologies to an eternally populated hell can be seen to betray an equally unstated conviction that God cannot, in fact, be truly and finally victorious over sin; that God cannot truly and finally *be God* in the face of sin. Rather, in many conservative theologies, sin takes on a power that exists outside and beyond the reach of God's eternal intention, will, and action. Sin becomes a power that successfully obstructs, resists, limits, and compromises—indeed, defeats—God's intention, will, and action; a power in the face of which a God who supposedly loves all creatures and wants all to be saved is powerless to prevent a good many, if not most of those beloved creatures, from being given up to sin's destructive forces to be devoured, lost for all eternity.[22]

---

21. See, for example: "It is . . . not out of any kind of weakness, but in the relentless vindication and exercise of His righteousness that God, in electing, is merciful towards the creature, espousing its cause, giving to it in its poverty, need and suffering His own substance, creating its righteousness, guaranteeing its future . . . *He avenges sin not by regarding but by forgiving it* . . . The righteousness of God in His election means, then, that as a righteous Judge God perceives and estimates as such the lost case of the creature, and that in spite of its opposition He gives sentence in its favour, fashioning for it His own righteousness. It means that God does not acquiesce in the creature's self-destruction as its own enemy. He sees to it that His own prior claim on the creature . . . is not rendered null and void . . . We cannot distinguish God's kingly righteousness from His mercy. We need not deny it for the sake of His mercy" (Barth, *Dogmatics* II/2, 33–34; my emphasis).

22. See, for example, "The Determination of the Rejected," in *Dogmatics* II/2, 449–506. See especially, the passage on the open situation of proclamation: "But nothing else may be expected or conjectured of any rejected [e.g., Judas] than that in his place, by God's wonderful reversal as it was accomplished in Jesus Christ, an elect will one day stand" (Barth, *Dogmatics* II/2, 476–80).

As I have hinted at before, this conservative limiting of God's grace and genuflecting before the power of sin plays out in two primary ways. The Reformed traditions tend to limit God's gracious work and gift of salvation by limiting the number of folks God elects to receive that salvation, leaving the rest of sinful humanity to receive their just desserts. Other traditions (Arminian, Wesleyan, Roman Catholic) tend to limit God's grace by investing creaturely freedom and agency with a divine-like power over the eternal meaning and future of creaturely life, a power that not only competes with but eternally obstructs and overturns God's eternal and concrete intention, will, and action for the salvation of *all* creatures. The creature's sinful no to God proves to be finally more powerful than the divine Yes of God's eternal will, desire, and work for the salvation of all. In all of these traditions, the result is the same. God's grace—and the goodness of the news—is radically limited by our need to have someone get what they deserve by burning in hell for all eternity.

While perhaps less obvious, we must not think that liberal or progressive theologies are without their own forms of limiting the grace of God. With regard to the grace at work in salvation, this is most obvious in the very appropriate offence taken at the thought of there being a place at the cosmic wedding feast for unrepentant—or even repentant—perpetrators of unjust violence and cruelty. If there is no just come-uppance for the unjust oppressor, how good can the news really be for the victims of injustice and oppression? And in terms of the wider, more fundamental ways in which grace is essentially related to divine *freedom* in Barth's theology: liberal and progressive theologies cannot bear a God that is free—free from their criteria of proper divinity, and so from their veto power—any more than conservative theologies. As I've already suggested, a God that is free from theologically progressive approval and authorization, and from the progressive ethics understood to be the content and criteria of all proper, viable religion, is a God that can only be experienced as a danger and a threat. A good liberal or progressive wouldn't trust such a God as far as they could throw them. God must be kept tightly under the strict control of our best, most recent and sophisticated philosophical conceptualizing and theorizing, our most refined cultural and aesthetic sensibilities, and/or our best, most progressive ethical visions and commitments.

So, Is Barth a Universalist?

Does Barth, then, affirm a doctrine of universal salvation? If the reader is guessing that the answer—or at least *my* answer—to this question will be something like, "Well, yes and no, but ultimately, yes," then they have been paying attention!

Yes and no. Yes, because of God's eternal, sovereign, and irrevocable decision to be God only *for* the creature and all creation in Jesus (through the Spirit), the last, first. As we have seen, there is no God for whom No is God's first or final word to the creature. In Jesus Christ (through the Spirit), God's first and final word to and for the creature and all creation is Yes, and no one is excluded from the embrace of this eternal divine Yes. This is the unqualifiable, intractable, and irreversible universality of Barth's vision of the salvation eternally willed and made concretely actual in Jesus (thorough the Spirit). *All*—truly all: humanity, the world, and all creation; but note, *the last, first!*—are objectively saved in Jesus (through the Spirit) in as much as God's first and final decision, Word, and act to and for them is Yes and not No.

However, the answer must initially include an albeit provisional, ultimately bracketed no for two reasons. First, this is due to Barth's commitment to divine freedom. Barth refuses the moniker of universalist. He denies that his view of salvation is a doctrine of universal*ism*—Barth cites the technical term, *apokatastasis*. For Barth, what these terms traditionally imply would impinge upon the freedom of divine will, decision, and action. And as we have seen, Barth understands divine freedom to be absolutely fundamental to the goodness of the gospel. For Barth, the freedom in which God is with and for us all in Jesus (through the Spirit), the last, first, issues a constriction upon theological speculation in this regard. We are prevented from implying or claiming any *necessity* to the final outcome of the history initiated by and made actual in God's eternal will, decision, Word, and act that is Jesus Christ (in the Spirit). *We* cannot know in advance, with the certainty of any absolute calculation or necessity *of ours*, what this final outcome will be.

One is tempted to say that the second reason for the provisional—yet real; not ephemeral—no is due to Barth's accompanying commitment to *creaturely* freedom. However, this would create confusion with regard to Barth's counterintuitive view of genuine creaturely freedom, a view we will try to at least catch a glimpse of in chapter 6. Suffice it to say, for Barth, the reality and power of sin finds expression in the creaturely no of resistance to the divine Yes. As such, sin involves an albeit non-necessary expression of the genuine *otherness* of creaturely reality created by God. However, it cannot be seen as an expression of genuine creaturely *freedom*. Sin can only be an expression of creaturely bondage, not creaturely freedom. For Barth, genuine creaturely freedom is always freedom *from* the bondage of sin, never freedom *to* sin. Creaturely freedom to sin would be a contradiction in terms; much like an alcoholic's freedom to drink. An alcoholic is only free by saying *no* to a drink, not in being able to say *either yes or no* to a drink; because saying yes to a drink is simply an expression of their bondage, of their *lack* of freedom. More on this later.

In light of this briefest of prefatory glimpses of Barth on creaturely freedom, it would be more accurate to say that our answer to the question of whether Barth is a universalist must include a provisional no because of his commitment to the genuine, concrete *otherness* of the creature in relation to God and the very real reality of sin as the creaturely no of resistance to the divine Yes. For Barth, we must take the reality of the creaturely no to God seriously. We are not free to imply or claim an inevitable, necessary rescinding of that no by the creature in the context of eternity; we simply do not possess the capacity for this kind of knowledge, to know for certain that a creaturely no to God will not have the stamina to continue to flee from God's pursuit throughout all eternity. The situation between the divine Yes of God to and for the creature in Jesus (through the Spirit) and the no of the creature to God that is taken to the grave and into eternity must remain *open*, for Barth, at least *for us*. We are not free to finally resolve that stand-off in either direction according to what we might feel to be a theological or ethical necessity.[23]

But ultimately, yes. I believe the answer regarding Barth and universal salvation must ultimately conclude with a yes, albeit an eschatologically open yes. And this is simply because, for Barth, the stand-off between God's divine Yes to the creature in Jesus (through the Spirit) and the creature's creaturely no to God is simply not a fair fight. The former constitutes the very ground, possibility, meaning, and boundary of the latter. For Barth, Christians and churches can never—or *should* never—believe in or bet on the creaturely no. They can and should always only believe in and bet on—indeed, live in

---

23. See, for example, Barth, *Dogmatics* II/2, 417ff. See especially: "If we are to respect the freedom of divine grace, we cannot venture the statement that it must and will finally be coincident with the world of man as such (as in the doctrine of the so-called *apokatastasis*). No such right or necessity can legitimately be deduced . . . [God's] election and calling do not give rise to any historical metaphysics, but only to the necessity of attesting them on the ground that they have taken place in Jesus Christ and His community. But, again . . . *we cannot venture the opposite statement that there cannot and will not be this final opening up and enlargement of the circle of election and calling* . . . We would be developing an opposing historical metaphysics if we were to try to attribute any limits—and therefore an end of these frontier-crossings—to the loving-kindness of God" (Barth, *Dogmatics* II/2, 417; my emphasis).

real hope and expectation that the final outcome will be determined by—the eternal divine Yes.[24]

LOOKING FORWARD: WE DO STUFF TOO

In light of everything we have seen so far, and especially in this chapter, one can be forgiven for wondering if Barth's theology is always and only about God, despite my occasional efforts to suggest otherwise. When reading Barth, God certainly can appear to be doing all the work.

While ultimately a caricature, this is not entirely off base. From Barth's point of view, liberal theology had lost its way by making Christian faith and theology all about *us*. The needed corrective involved rediscovering God as the main character of the gospel story. The prepositional phrase, *from God*, with its theological logic and order signaling the primacy of God's free, initiating will, decision, and action in all things, does indeed function as a helpful signpost for charting the central themes and movements of Barth's theological vision. However, what Barth sees as the appropriate primacy of God as the primary acting subject in the gospel story does *not*, in fact, entirely eclipse the status and role of the creature. It does not mean that God is the *only* actor in the story. We will look more closely at the creature's role in the story in the last couple of chapters.

In this chapter, we have mainly been discussing themes traditionally having to do with the doctrine of God—divine transcendence, sovereignty, freedom, mystery, and grace—as they are determined in and by the fundamental movement of Barth's theological logic. The reader may have noticed that it was impossible to talk about any of these dimensions of who God is, at least as Barth understands them, apart from the concrete way in which Barth believes God has given Godself to the creature to be known and loved in the personal reality, history, event, and relation that is God for us in Jesus (through the Spirit), the last, first. Indeed, for Barth, the only reason we know

---

24. Again, see Barth, *Dogmatics* II/2, 476–80, on the open situation of proclamation and the stand-off between Jesus's divine Yes to Judas and Judas's creaturely no to Jesus. See also: "The mutual indwelling or union of the divine and human possibility, of man's knowing and his being known by God, is an event in the freedom of man, and yet . . . it cannot in any sense be regarded as its product . . . man must be set aside and God Himself presented as the original subject, as the primary power, as the creator of the possibility of knowledge of God's Word. Christ does not remain outside. And it is true enough that man must open the door (Rev. 3:20). But the fact that this takes place is *quoad actum* [with regard to the act] and *quoad potentiam* [with regard to the power/possibility] the work of the Christ who stands outside. *Hence it is also unconditionally true that the risen Christ passes though closed doors* (Jn. 20:19f)" (Barth, *Dogmatics* I/1, 247; my emphasis).

that knowledge of and relation to God comes to us always and only *from God* is because of the way God has in fact already concretely come to us and given Godself wholly and fully to us: in Jesus Christ (through the power of the Spirit). It is to this concreteness of God's self-disclosing self-giving that we now turn in a more intentional and focused way.

QUESTIONS

1. How does *from God*, as the movement of Barth's theological logic, determine his corrective to liberal theology as an explicit *reversal* of the movement of the latter's approach to theology and faith? Can you give some particular examples?

2. How and why can Barth's view of divine sovereignty and omnipotence be distinguished from what progressive theologies rightly critique as traditional—and destructive—views of absolute divine power, and what Barth himself critiques as "abstract" and "naked" divine power?

3. How does Barth's *from God* (a) ensure that the Word of God, together with the divine-human relation enacted in and by it, are never our possession or at our disposal, while *also* (b) affirming the good news that God does truly give Godself to us to be known and loved in a very concrete way?

4. Relatedly, how does Barth's view of divine mystery differ from how that theological term is traditionally understood and employed to signify the ultimate unknowability of God? How is Barth's view of divine freedom related to this distinctive view of divine mystery?

5. How is Barth able to affirm a universal breadth of God's saving action in Jesus Christ (through the Spirit) and yet say he is not affirming a doctrine of universal*ism* as an absolute theological principle or necessity?

5

THE CONCRETENESS OF BARTH'S THEOLOGICAL LOGIC
—Only *in Jesus Christ*

FOR BARTH, WE ONLY know and have God—and ourselves, and the world—*from God*, in the particular, concrete divine self-giving that is God for us all in Jesus (through the Spirit), the last, first. This means we cannot escape the corollary: we know and have God—and ourselves—*only* in Jesus Christ (through the Spirit). With this *only* we find ourselves back where we started. It is a place that we have, in fact, never really left. This is appropriate for any reading of Barth, for it is fundamental to his own theology that in all things, no matter what is under consideration, Christians and churches must continually return to what Barth believes to be the beginning of all things, the beginning that is God's first Word in relation to all that is not God: not "Let there be light!" but "Jesus Christ!"[1]

---

1. See, for example: "That other to which God stands in relationship . . . is not simply and directly the created world as such. There is, too, a relationship of God to the world . . . There is a history between God and the world. But this history has no independent signification. It takes place in the interests of the primal history which is played out between God and this one man and his people . . . The partner of God . . . is the one man Jesus and the people represented in Him. Only secondarily, and for His sake, is it 'man,' and 'humanity' and the whole remaining cosmos" (Barth, *Dogmatics* II/2, 7–8).

CHRISTOCENTRISM, YES—BUT WITH A TRINITARIAN BREADTH AND UNIVERSAL EMBRACE

We are now in a position to revisit the issue of Barth's Christocentrism in a little more depth, together with the critiques that come from both the theological left and right.[2] When Barth says that God wills only one thing and says only one Word from and for all eternity and in the midst of history, and that that one will and Word is to be God wholly and only with, for, and as the creature in Jesus (through the Spirit), the last, first, it is difficult *not* to feel that he is collapsing the whole perplexing biblical narrative and Trinitarian doctrinal inheritance into a single moment and a single doctrine: Christology's description of the person and work of Jesus in his Incarnation, life, death, and resurrection.

As I have already noted, Barth's almost perseverative focus on Jesus Christ is critiqued by conservatives as well as progressives for losing sight of the vast expanse of the ineffable mystery of divine nature and essence in God's eternal being, and the breadth and depth of that God's engagement with creation. For conservatives in particular, lost is the long and complicated history of God's journey with Israel; the life and ministry of the church, its polity and authority; the individual's life of faith; the distinctive work of the Holy Spirit; and the juicy details of the last judgment with its horrific torments of eternal hellfire alongside the bliss of an eternity in heaven. For progressives in particular, lost are the infinite number of ways in which God is available to *all* creatures and communities throughout history and across the globe, on their own terms and in their own stories and experience, apart from and independent of the Abraham-Israel-Jesus-church business; the depth and riches available through the myriad religious experiences and religious and intellectual traditions throughout history and across the globe; the many possibilities of mutuality, inter-dependence, and partnership with the church's many neighbors of differing religious, cultural, and intellectual traditions. So much of the biblical and Trinitarian doctrinal inheritance, not to mention the vast array of human religious experience, seems to be excluded if all we know of God and of ourselves is contained in this one Word, this one name and title: Jesus Christ.

Here again, there is important truth in the critiques. Though, at this point, I hope the reader can begin to anticipate how Barth might respond

---

2. For work on conservative critiques of Barth's Christocentrism, see Bolich, *Barth and Evangelicalism*; Thorne, *Evangelicalism and Barth*. See especially, Gibson and Strange, *Engaging with Barth*, 26–27, 272, 339. For the logic of the liberal critique, see Tillich on Jesus as the Christ and the end of Jesusology in Tillich, *Systematic Theology* I, 135ff.

or how one might respond when thinking with Barth. This is not to say that such a response would thoroughly address the critiques to the satisfaction of the critics. It *is* to say that such a response would help clarify what is and what is not risked in Barth's Chrisocentrism, what it is exactly that *is* excluded and what it is exactly that is *included* by and in it. It is to say that such a response would help ensure that the critiques themselves do not lose sight of the full depth and breadth of the Trinitarian, universalist dimensions of Barth's distinctive Christocentrism.

It is true, the Christocentrism of Barth's "*only* in Jesus Christ" exerts a very concrete *constriction* upon Christian faith and theology, upon not only what is and can be known of God and the human being and their relation, but also upon God's very being and action. Consequently, Barth's theology does indeed *risk* all of the problematic exclusions mentioned above and called out by his conservative and progressive critics. These need to be taken seriously in any assessment of Barth's theology. If all these exclusions are truly in effect in the straightforward way the critics say they are, that would be a serious problem indeed.

However, as we might now suspect, an informed understanding of what Barth means by Jesus Christ (in the Spirit) and all that is *included* in this name and title, as the one eternal divine will, decision, Word, and act—person, event, history, and relation—made concrete in history, for all of history, may reveal that the exclusions named above are in need of serious qualification. What is included and made necessary in and by the "*only* in Jesus Christ" may involve quite radical forms of *openness, expansion, and inclusion* that accompany and complicate the constriction of Barth's Christocentrism. Similarly, the distinctiveness of Barth's Christocentrism may throw certain of these conservative and progressive concerns themselves into specific relief, suggesting they may be rooted in assumptions and investments that could themselves be seen as questionable or problematic, at least from a certain view of the gospel and its relation to Christian faith and theology.

In what follows, we will look more closely at what actually *is* excluded in and by the "*only* in Jesus Christ," at least from what I believe to be Barth's point of view, together with all that is definitely *included* and made necessary in and by this *only*. Ultimately, of course, it must be up to the reader to come to their own assessment of Barth's distinctive form of Trinitarian, universalist Christocentrism, and whether it's a risk worth taking, or as I think Barth would see it, a risk that *must* be taken. I will first address the key *methodological* issues involved in Barth's "*only* in Jesus Christ," then turn to address the issues of confessional and doctrinal *content*.

"ONLY IN JESUS CHRIST" AS METHODOLOGICAL CONSTRAINT

"We begin with Jesus Christ."[3] We have already caught glimpses of the counterintuitive nature of Barth's approach to the *way* of the church's theological thinking. It is a way dictated by what Barth believes to be the one eternal will, decision, Word, and act of God to be wholly and only with and for us in Jesus (through the Spirit), the last, first; a will, decision, Word, and act that is the source, content, and meaning of all God's dealings with creation and so the source, content, and criteria of all the church's speaking and acting in and for the world. The theological logic of this way of thinking and doing theology runs against the grain of our natural habits of thinking, both in terms of the traditional theological thinking of the church and of traditional philosophical thinking in the West. As I said at the outset, this is one of the key reasons why Barth's theology—and myself, in trying to introduce that theology—is constantly repeating itself. There is a need to continually remind the reader—and myself!—of this counterintuitive logic. *Deeply ingrained habits of thinking are hard to break.* And breaking long-ingrained habits of thinking—breaking open, breaking in, interrupting, confronting, addressing—is precisely what Barth believes the one Word of God that is Jesus Christ (in the Spirit) does to and for us. Attempting to point to, remind of, and prepare for this in-breaking and breaking open is precisely what Barth believes the church's theology is called to do. This involves several methodological constraints by which, according to Barth, the church's theological thinking and speaking is to be ordered and determined, if it is to be faithful in this effort.

Special Revelation as Context for General Revelation

For Barth, "*only* in Jesus Christ" reverses the theological ordering of what the church has traditionally called natural revelation and special revelation that has been assumed as normative throughout most of the church's theological history. Traditionally, the church has affirmed both natural (or general) revelation and special revelation as means for true knowledge of God, the former providing a general, philosophical knowledge of God's existence and some basic characteristics of the nature of divine being (e.g., God is perfect, one, simple, eternal, immutable [unchanging], impassable [unaffectable], the "omnis"—omnipresent, omniscient, etc.), and that we as mortal and finite human creatures cannot measure up to such a God. This knowledge can be affirmed as true, grounded as it is in God's self-revelation through creation

---

3. Barth, *Dogmatics* IV/3, 38. We encounter forms of this sentence in each volume of the *Church Dogmatics*.

The Concreteness of Barth's Theological Logic

and reason (so that no one will be "without excuse" before God [Rom 1:20]), but it is not sufficient for salvation.

Traditionally, natural revelation does not include knowledge of the gospel news about the distinctive nature of sin (beyond mere finitude) and what the creator God has done to make provision for salvation. Special revelation is required for this kind of saving knowledge of the gospel—knowledge that we are not only finite, but sinful, and in need of a particular form of salvation; and that God is our savior, partner, and friend as well as our creator and judge. This knowledge is made available to us through God's specific, revelatory self-giving to the creature in the history of God's engagement with creation beyond creating and sustaining the cosmos. Most specifically, it is traditionally believed that this history is none other than the particular history of God's journey with the people of Israel among the nations, for the sake of the nations, given witness in the Hebrew Scriptures and the Christian New Testament. It is a *continuing* history whose goal and meaning—at least for traditional Christian faith and theology—is ultimately expressed and secured in the event of God's unique and fully incarnate presence in the birth, life, death, resurrection, and ascension of Jesus (in the power of the Spirit), with and for Israel and the nations, as the promised Messiah of Israel and the reconciliation and redemption of a world caught in the grip of sin and the power of death.

So goes the traditional Christian consensus on the two forms of revelation and how they are related. They are both seen as true, and both are seen as necessary, but they are not seen as equal. Furthermore, natural revelation is generally addressed first in theological work, as a baseline of true but general (and non-salvific) knowledge about God that Christians share with everybody else. Everybody, simply by being human, is believed to have—via reason and/or certain forms of experience—this baseline knowledge of the true God. This knowledge is seen to function as the ground upon which the faith that comes with special revelation and a hearing of the gospel—*if* one is lucky enough to hear it, *and* smart enough to respond appropriately—can then be built.

Barth diverges from this traditional consensus in two interrelated ways. First and most striking, Barth rejects the idea of a natural revelation that can give true, albeit limited and provisional, knowledge of the true God independent of an event of free, revelatory divine self-giving by the God who has from all eternity determined to be God *only* in being with and for the creature in Jesus (through the Spirit); that is, apart from or before an event of special revelation. For Barth, our only knowledge of the true God comes when God speaks and acts in an event of personal divine self-giving; that is, in the Trinitarian event that is God for us all in Jesus (through the Spirit), the last, first. Put differently, Barth grounds the church's knowledge of God solely in the event of special revelation. Strictly speaking, for Barth, there is no natural or general revelation *that can function as the ground for true, albeit limited and provisional, knowledge of the true God.* This would constitute a form of what Barth calls natural theology: knowledge of God based on natural or general creaturely capacities and possibilities independent of a free event of God's own self-giving in concrete speaking and acting. We have already discussed Barth's rejection of natural theology and the fundamental reasons for that rejection.

Methodologically, then—and here is the second point—Barth *begins and ends* the theological enterprise with special revelation as the sole ground for the Christian's and the church's knowledge of God. Barth's *Church Dogmatics* begins with the Trinitarian event of the eternal-historical Word of God that is God only and wholly for us all in Jesus (through the Spirit), the last, first, as the basis of all the church's knowing, thinking, and speaking of God. The doctrine of the Word of God that constitutes the first volume of his *Church Dogmatics* doubles as Barth's doctrine of the Trinity. Only then does he move on to consider a doctrine of God, as a doctrine of *this particular* God: the triune God whose freedom for the creature in and for love is made concrete and actual in Jesus (through the Spirit), as given witness in the gospel.

Consequently, for Barth, there is not a moment wherein the church may consider any kind of God-in-general, wherein it may think or speak of God in a general way abstracted from the concrete reality and event that has occurred and does occur in God's revelatory self-giving in Jesus (through the Spirit). If the church must have a doctrine of God, complete with a list of divine attributes, the church can only ask what the traditional divine attributes might mean as applied to *this particular* God, the God who is already known as Trinitarian personal reality and relation, history and event, in and through the concrete history of God for us all in Jesus (through the Spirit), the last, first. As we have seen, Barth can and does speak of this particular God by employing the traditional divine attributes of transcendence and sovereignty—and, with care, even omnipotence. However, those attributes mean very different things when employed in relation to the God known fully in the manger, the marginalized community, the table fellowship, and the cross of Jesus (through the Spirit)—that is, known in special revelation—than when applied to a God known through the cosmic powers and glories of creation and the sophistications of philosophical reflection on the necessary nature of divine essence.

However, for Barth, this does *not* mean that there is no such thing as natural revelation in the sense of creation proclaiming the glory of God.⁴ Barth's grounding of our knowledge of God solely in special revelation means that we only understand the true glory of God that creation is proclaiming when we *already* know that God to be the God who has determined and given Godself fully, from all eternity, as God only and wholly with and for the creature in Jesus (through the Spirit), the last, first—and here, *the last, first*, is essential for Barth. That is, when the divine glory that nature proclaims is seen in light of the concrete event of special revelation that occurs in Jesus Christ (through the Spirit), that glory can never be mistaken for an omnipotence resonant with cosmic power. The glory of God is only known when it is consistent with and expressible in the vulnerability of the manger; the risky company of marginalized communities; the hospitality, generosity, and laughter of table fellowship; the solidarity and suffering of the cross; and the righteous justice of the temple cleanser, the breaker of religious laws, the unpious friend of sinners.

For Barth, whatever room is made for natural revelation in our theological thinking, it can only *follow* and be *grounded in* special revelation, methodologically. Its meaning can only be thoroughly and concretely determined by special revelation; that is, by what we know of God in God's self-giving in Jesus Christ (through the Spirit). Special revelation is the context for natural revelation, not vice versa; the tables are turned, the direction reversed. Again, Barth turns the tables on tradition as well as on modern liberal theology. He reverses the order and direction of the movement of our traditional habits of theological thinking. Or, more accurately, Barth calls attention to the reversal

---

4. See, for example: "[T]hey ['the people of Christ'] know only those words and works and things which *by their negation are sign-posts* to the Holy One" (Barth, *Romans*, 36; my emphasis); "To those who have abandoned direct communication, the communication is made. To those willing to venture with God, He speaks. Those who take upon them the divine 'No' shall themselves be borne by the greater divine 'Yes'" (Barth, *Romans*, 41); "[A]ll experience bears within it an understanding by which it is itself condemned, and ... all time bears within it that eternity by which it is dissolved. Judgement is not annihilation; by it all things are established" (Barth, *Romans*, 79); "Their theme [the prophets]—and it is the proper theme of history ... is concerned with the perception of the uncertainty of men in relation to what they are not, that is to say, in their relation to God ... They allow full right to the materialistic, secular, 'sceptical' [*sic*] view of the world; and then, assuming this final skepticism, they set forth upon the road which leads to the knowledge of God and thereby to the knowledge of the eternal significance of the world and of history. No road to the eternal meaning of the created world has ever existed, save the road of negation. This is the lesson of history" (Barth, *Romans*, 87).

he believes to be *enacted and determined by God*—the God who has spoken and acted decisively and definitely and who continues to speak and act in the eternal-historical Trinitarian event of self-determination, self-giving, and self-revelation that is God for us all in Jesus (through the Spirit), the last, first.

Liberal and progressive theologies diverge from the traditional consensus on revelation in the opposite direction: for liberals and progressives, *all* revelation is *natural* revelation. For liberal and progressive theologies, what tradition refers to as special revelation is, in fact, only a distinctive way of talking that the church has developed in order to speak about and symbolically express its own particular experience of *natural* revelation. It is a way to symbolically express the church's distinctive experience of the divine presence universally available in and to all creation as personal in nature, as God speaking and acting. It is not to be understood as a literal description of God *actually* speaking and acting; we experience God *as if* God was speaking and acting in a personal way, i.e., like we do, i.e., anthropomorphically.

Liberal and progressive theologies understand the church's employment of "Word of God" language to be our distinctive way of speaking symbolically, i.e., religiously, to ourselves about ourselves, about certain distinctive dimensions of our natural yet historically determined, and so distinct and particular, religious experience of divine presence. This is a divine presence that is universal, immanent in and to all creation, and so available to all; it is experienced in many different ways and symbolically expressed through many different cultural histories, practices, and symbol systems (from the liberal and progressive point of view).[5] And not all of these ways involve the personal, for example, the personal relation of speaking and intentional action. Consequently, a central pillar of liberal and progressive theology: symbolic expression of our religious experiences of divine presence is *not* to be mistaken for literal description of who or what God actually *is*—or does—*in Godself*. Whereas for Barth, the gospel is not a particular instance of the general category of religious symbolic expression, but a strange piece of apostolic news, a report that God has actually, concretely *given* Godself to be known *as God is in Godself*.

---

5. More recent progressive theologies have begun to entertain the possibility that the multiplicity of religions reflects a corresponding multiplicity of divine or ultimate realities. This is, at least in some measure, a critical recognition that to assume one universal divine reality behind all religious traditions and experience is still too much of an imperialistic imposition upon and erasure of genuine religious difference. See Philip Clayton's critique of John Hick, a leading voice in the "one universal divine reality" approach: Clayton, "God Who Is (Not) One," 19–37.

The Particular as the Context for the Universal

Barth's reversal of the traditional relation between natural and special revelation is part and parcel of his wider reversal of the traditional philosophical relation between the universal and the particular in Western habits of thinking. The logic of Barth's theology not only moves against the grain of the church's traditional, normative ways of thinking and working theologically, but also moves against the grain of the West's traditional, normative ways of thinking and working philosophically. This is not accidental: the history of the church's normative way of thinking and working theologically, at least in the Roman Catholic and Protestant traditions, has been, from at least the second century (but also already visible in Paul),[6] closely tied to and influenced by—though not in every instance absolutely determined by—the history of the West's normative ways of thinking and working philosophically.

Throughout the long history of Western philosophy, the Western mind has been formed to think of the universal as the appropriate context in which to consider the nature, meaning, and significance of the particular. The truth of a particular reality is properly understood when appropriately placed and considered within its wider context, within a more general or universal category or concept. Think, for example, of the relation between genus and species: the latter are properly known and understood *within* the context of the former, their general category of commonality, as particular instances of the former. *Contra* this commonsense thinking, Barth argues that, *in the particular case of the gospel*—that is, not as a general rule or necessary principle, but in the concrete, radically contingent case of what actually occurs in Jesus Christ (through the Spirit)—the particular is the context of and for the universal. That is, the meaning of all history and all creation is determined by and comprehended within the eternally willed and concretely actual history that is the Trinitarian event of God for us all in Jesus (through the Spirit), the last, first.[7] Put differently, to understand the meaning of creation, you must begin with the promise and reality of redemption (see the following section); within the context of the Hebrew Bible (at least as read by Barth), to properly understand the meaning of Genesis, you must begin with Exodus; within

---

6. See Reuther, *Faith and Fratricide*.

7. See, for example: "The general (the world or man) exists for the sake of the particular. In the particular the general has its meaning and fulfilment . . . Everything which comes from God takes place 'in Jesus Christ' . . ." (Barth, *Dogmatics* II/2, 8); "He does the general for the sake of the particular. Or to put it in another way, He does the general through the particular, and in and with it. That is God according to His self-revelation" (Barth, *Dogmatics* II/2, 53).

the context of the church's doctrinal thinking—again, when thinking with Barth—one begins with the strange and unaccountable apostolic confessions about Jesus and works backwards to a doctrine of God (and to everything else).

The Work of Theology Is Bound, Constrained, and Determined by Its Object

Finally, then, for Barth, the way and work of Christian theology is fundamentally constrained and constricted in very particular and concrete ways. It is not primarily an exercise of free thinking or creative writing. Christian theology is *given* its object, its subject matter—for Barth: the Word of God that is God only and wholly for us in Jesus (through the Spirit), the last, first—from the outset and from the outside, as it were.[8] The work of theology is confronted by its object, interrupted by it, claimed and commissioned by it, beholden to and determined by it from first to last. It is told what it must say and can say, and what it must not say and cannot say. The object or subject matter of Christian faith and theology is not of its own making, does not well up naturally from within the human breast, demanding creative expression. It is not our idea. Christian faith and theology is more about attempting to point faithfully away from itself to its given object—to that which addresses it, determines it, and calls it into being—than about so-called free creative expression. As Kierkegaard suggests, Christian faith is not strictly an aesthetic enterprise. It is a much more mundane—and democratic—reality. In fact, anyone can do it, regardless of aesthetic or poetic ability or inclination, even the lowly shoe cobbler or cheese monger.[9]

However, as we noted in the first chapter, and as we will see again in the following two chapters, this does *not* mean that there is no room for creaturely creativity in the life and work of Christian faith and theology. One only need look at Barth's own radically innovative doctrine of election for an example of such creaturely theological creativity. The one living Word of God, spoken in freedom and heard anew in a history of free events of divine-human

---

8. See, for example, Barth, *Dogmatics* II/1, 3–10. See especially: "But the fulfilling of the knowledge of God with which we are now concerned most certainly does not rest on a free choice of this or that object, of this or that 'God' . . . everything that is described as 'God' on the basis of a free choice cannot possibly be God . . . The knowledge of God with which we are here concerned takes place, not in a free choice, but with a very definite constraint. It stands or falls with its one definite object . . . Because it is bound to God's Word . . . the knowledge of God with which we are here concerned is bound to the God who in His Word gives Himself to the Church to be known as God" (Barth, Dogmatics II/1, 6–7).

9. I have much to say about Kierkegaard in this regard, in an obviously Barthian reading of his work. See Boesel, *In Kierkegaard's Garden*.

encounter, calls for an illimitable number of creaturely words and actions in the response of faithful witness in and for an illimitable number of concrete contexts.

THE THEOLOGICAL CONTENT OF THE *ONLY*: RADICAL PARTICULARITY AS RADICAL INCLUSION

We now turn from the specific methodological constraints imposed by the "*only* in Jesus Christ" upon the church's *way* of thinking and speaking theologically, determining the theological logic of its faith and theology, to the ways in which this *only* determines the *content* of what the church actually says and does—or *should* say and do, according to Barth. In keeping with our theme of how Barth's theology cuts both ways, to the left and to the right, we will look at the paradoxical way in which its "*only* in Jesus Christ" both narrows (*contra* liberal theologies) and widens (*contra* conservative theologies) the scope of the gospel. We will look at the two primary dimensions of Barth's theological vision of and commitment to the *only*: (a) what the church must say about God, and what the church is prevented from saying about God; (b) what the church must say about the creature in relation to this God, and what the church is prevented from saying about the creature in this relation. The chapter concludes by looking at the implications of Barth's "*only* in Jesus Christ" for the church's reading of Scripture and the problem of Christian supersessionism.

God—*Only* in Jesus Christ

Perhaps the clearest and most thoroughgoing articulation of both the decisive exclusion and the comprehensive, unqualifiable inclusion that occurs in the *only* of Barth's "*only* in Jesus Christ" can be found in his mature doctrine of God. As we have already seen, for Barth, this means that the traditional divine attributes typically found in a Christian doctrine of God can only mean what they mean as determined by who we know God to be in God's concrete self-giving and self-disclosure in Jesus (through the Spirit). As Barth puts it, they cannot be general theological or philosophical concepts applied to God prior to or independent of the concrete content of the gospel.[10] That is, what

---

10. See, for example: "The recognition of divine attributes *cannot be taken to mean that for us God is subsumed under general notions, under the loftiest ideas of our knowledge of creaturely reality*, and that He participates in its perfections. It is not that we recognize and acknowledge the infinity, justice, wisdom, etc. of God *because we already know from other sources what all this means and we apply it to God* in an eminent sense, thus fashioning for

they mean in the context of Christian faith is not necessarily the same as what they mean in other contexts, be those contexts religious, philosophical, cultural, or aesthetic. Again, the divine power and authority implied in concepts like transcendence, sovereignty, and omnipotence can only mean what they mean for Christian faith in the radical divine vulnerability of the manger, the marginalized company, the table fellowship, and the cross of Jesus (in the Spirit); in the radical divine self-giving for the sake of concrete relations of communion, fellowship, and mutual blessing wherein the last are first. (Though, again, and as we will see in the following chapters, Barth does not emphasize these particular material dimensions of the divine self-giving that occurs in Jesus and are signaled in "the last, first," as often or as loudly as he could have done.)

It is in his doctrine of election—constituting the second part-volume of his doctrine of God in the *Church Dogmatics*—that Barth fleshes out the most radical implications of this epistemological limit of the "*only* in Jesus Christ" for the church's knowledge of God. We have already caught glimpses of how, for Barth, God does not merely choose to give and disclose Godself *to and for the creature* only and wholly in Jesus (through the Spirit). In that one will, decision, Word, and act, God, from all eternity, *determines and limits Godself* to be no other God and to be God in no other way than the God who is with, for, and as the creature. Consequently, because God has first and foremost *elected Godself* in this way, from all eternity, there simply *is no other God* than the God who has given and continues to give themself wholly and irrevocably to the creature in Jesus (through the Spirit) for concrete relations of love and responsibility in fellowship and communion, between God and creatures, and in God, between and among creatures, the last, first. The "*only* in Jesus Christ" is not simply an *epistemological* limit about what *we* can and cannot *know* about God. It is a self-imposed, self-determining albeit freely chosen limiting of *God's own self*, of *God's very identity and mode of being*.[11]

---

ourselves an image of God after the pattern of our image of the world, i.e. . . . after our own image . . . *There are not first of all power, goodness, knowledge, will, etc. in general, and then in particular God also as one of the subjects to whom all these things accrue as a predicate* . . . *Therefore God does not borrow what He is from outside, from some other*" (Barth, *Dogmatics* II/1, 333–34; my emphasis); "It is He, *this* God, who as the Lord and Shepherd of that people is also, of course, the World-ruler, the Creator of all things, the Controller of all events, both great and small. But in every way His government of the world is only the extension, the application and the development of His government in this one particular sphere" (Barth, *Dogmatics* II/2, 53; my emphasis).

11. See, for example, "The Place of the Doctrine in Dogmatics," in Barth, *Dogmatics* II/2, 76–93. See especially: "[I]n the primal and basic decision in which He wills to be and actually is God, in the mystery of what takes place from and to all eternity within

The Exclusionary Constriction of Particularity: What We Cannot Say

So what is excluded by the limit of this "*only* in Jesus Christ"? For starters, a positive doctrine of religious pluralism is excluded. We will explore the distinctive dimensions of this exclusion in more depth in chapter 7. But at this point, it is clear that, for Barth, we *cannot say* that some or all religions—including the Christian religion—function as salvific pathways to the divine apart from who God is and what God has done in Jesus (through the Spirit). If God *is* only in God's self-determining, revelatory act of self-giving to the creature for concrete relation in Jesus (through the Spirit), then all roads do not in fact lead to the top of the mountain, as the saying goes. Or, more accurately, all roads may indeed lead to the top of mountain, and the views up there may indeed be breathtaking, inspiring, far-reaching, and well-worth the climb, but the true and living God has long since vacated the premises for the depths of the deepest valleys and forgotten back alleys to seek the company of those who lack either the opportunity or the piety, the vacation time or the self-discipline, to even begin the ascent on *any* of the many roads—including the Christian road—leading up to the superior religious climes of the mountain top.

There is another side, then, to this particular coin of exclusion. There is simply no other God than the God who is eternally and concretely *for* the creature; indeed, precisely for *the lost and sinful creature*, regardless of religious, irreligious, or non-religious persuasion. Any God or any part of God that might be against the creature in its lostness and captivity to sin; that might mean the creature harm; that might not have its best interest at heart; that might be content to leave the creature, even one, the least deserving, wallowing in its self-incurred lostness and despair in the depths of the valley or the back alley; that might not go to the absolute furthest lengths to guarantee and secure the well-being of the creature; that would not let anything in heaven or on earth, even the creature's own frailty and resistance and commitment to self-harm, fundamentally threaten the existence of the creature; that might stop short of eternally and concretely claiming the creature as beloved child and partner for whom God's very self is given—*all this* is decisively *excluded* as even a hint of possibility. For Barth, there is simply no God nor any part of God that at any time or for any reason either wills or enacts harm upon or the destruction of the creature, not even when, in their lostness, frailty, and need, the creature's sole desire is to bring about and ensure their own

---

Himself, within His triune being, God is none other than the One who in His Son or Word *elects Himself*, and in and with Himself elects His people" (Barth, *Dogmatics* II/2, 77; my emphasis).

destruction. In Barth's theology, the church is forbidden to ever confess or proclaim—i.e., it *cannot say* it believes in—such a God. Unfortunately, from Barth's perspective, it is just such a God that the traditional church has almost always insisted on confessing and proclaiming.

The Inclusionary Universal Embrace: What We **Must** Say

Just as there is no *God* that is against the creature, even in their lostness and captivity to sin, there is no *creature*—lost, sinful, or otherwise—that is not *included* in the unequivocal, irrevocable, eternally willed Yes of God for the creature made concretely actual in Jesus Christ (through the Spirit). As we have seen, the concrete content of the eternal Yes of God to the creature, to be with, for, and as the creature, even in their lostness and captivity to sin, includes the full scope of God's Trinitarian engagement with the world from before creation through the *eschaton* to come. For Barth, then, to know and have God *only* in Jesus Christ does not mean that we know and have God only in and through *our belief* in Jesus. Rather, the *only* refers to the objective reality and history that is God for us in Jesus (through the Spirit) that Barth believes has in fact occurred and is in fact the case *for every creature and all creation* whether we know it or believe it or not. In whatever way and to whatever extent we know and have God, it is always *this* God that we know and have; it is always the result of and response to *being known by* this God, found and claimed by this God's free self-giving.

While all of this is included in what Barth understands to occur in the personal, eternal-historical event that is God only and wholly for us all in Jesus (through the Spirit), the last, first, he often works with a shorthand version of this content. He will refer to what occurs in Jesus Christ (through the Spirit) as the strictly irreversible movement from death to resurrection, from Good Friday to Easter Sunday, from death and judgment to resurrected and redeemed life with God, and in God, with the neighbor.[12] As we've seen,

---

12. See, for example, "The Eternal Will of God in the Election of Jesus Christ," in Barth, *Dogmatics* II/2, 145–94. See especially: "[W]e must oppose all those theories which presume an equilibrium of God's twofold will. For the only knowledge which we have of man's foreordination to evil and death is in the form in which God of His great mercy accepted it as His own portion and burden, removing it from us and refusing to let it be our foreordination in any form. That removing and refusing took place in Jesus Christ . . . Unequivocally, and without reserve or diminution, God has elected and ordained man to bear the image of this [God's own] glory. That and that alone is what we see and know in Jesus Christ in relation to man. The suffering borne on the cross of Golgotha by the son of man in unity with the Son of God . . . *is a stage on the road, an unavoidable point of transition*, to the glory of the resurrection" (Barth, *Dogmatics* II/2, 172–73; my emphasis). See

the divine wrath over and judgment upon sin that is executed once for all on the cross is for the sake of and always followed by the reality of resurrected, redeemed life with God and neighbor as the meaning and future of every sinful creature. No one is separated from or left out of this universal embrace of the eternal Yes of God made concretely actual in Jesus (through the Spirit). For Barth, the "*only* in Jesus Christ" guarantees and ensures that no creature—especially in their lostness and captivity to sin—should be the object of divine judgment as God's first and/or final word. It is this guarantee—this unadulterated, unqualified, and irrevocable Yes of God to each and every creature without shadow of limit—that Barth believes the "*only* in Jesus Christ" requires the church to say and to live. It is what the church *must* say and live in every moment of every context. Unfortunately, from Barth's perspective, it is this very guarantee, this unqualifiable and irrevocable divine Yes to all, to each and every one, the last, first, that the traditional church has almost always failed or refused to say and live.

The Human Creature—*Only* in Jesus Christ

For Barth, what occurs in Jesus Christ (through the Spirit) is not just about who *God* is and what *God* does. It is also about who *we* are and what *we* do. What takes place in Jesus (through the Spirit) is not only God's Yes to the creature, but also the eternally willed creaturely yes back to God, and in this yes to God, a yes to the neighbor, the last, first, as the meaning and content of creaturely life.

One way in which Barth can be seen to be thinking in continuity *with* the orthodox doctrinal tradition is in his use of the Chalcedonian Christological formula regarding the identity of Jesus: fully God, fully human, two natures in one person. Consequently, for Barth, the one Word of God that is Jesus Christ (in the Spirit) tells us what it means—and what it does not mean—to be a human creature. For Barth, the one Word of God that is God for us all in Jesus (through the Spirit), the last, first, includes the responding, creaturely word that is the fully human Jesus's yes back to and for God. For Barth, Jesus is the only human being who says and lives an unequivocal and

---

also: "The shadow is itself sinister and threatening and dangerous and deadly enough. Yet it is this within the limit set for it by God . . . And this is its divinely imposed limit . . . that the rejected man exists in the person of Jesus Christ only in such a way that he is assumed into His being as the elect and beloved of God . . . only in such sort that as he is accepted and received by Him he is transformed, being put to death as the rejected and raised to his proper life as the elect, holy, justified and blessed . . . With Jesus Christ the rejected can only *have been* rejected. He cannot *be* rejected any more" (Barth, *Dogmatics* II/2, 453).

irrevocable creaturely yes back to God, who is wholly and fully *for God*—and in God, for the neighbor, the last, first—as the entire meaning and content of their creaturely life. As such, Jesus is the one human creature who lives as the creature they were created to be. This is because, for Barth, the nature and meaning of the human creature as eternally willed and concretely created by God is inhabited as the *act* of freely responding to God's Yes with a creaturely yes as the content of one's entire life, to whatever extent that action is possible for any given creature.[13] The full reality of human being is not exhausted in the metaphysical, ontological, biological, or cosmological structures of creation. Rather, it *occurs*—albeit in the context of those structures—as a personal, relational *event*. One gestures to the human creature one was created to be in the event of responding to God's Yes with one's own creaturely yes to God—as the content of one's whole life, in word and deed—and in that yes, a yes to one's neighbor, the last, first (to whatever extent that intentional decision and action of yes is possible for any given creature).

In Barth's theology, Jesus's creaturely yes to God is no historical accident, but the concrete actualization of God's eternal will for the creature and the internal rationale of all creation. Consequently, Jesus says and lives—enacts and actualizes—this creaturely yes to God *for us*. His creaturely yes is our creaturely yes. As a wholly and truly unqualified human creaturely yes to God, it is the yes determining the meaning and reality of all creaturely life, of each and every one.[14]

---

13. I am indebted to Max Thornton for recently helping me see more clearly the way in which issues of ability and ableism lie at the heart of theological and religious visions of the image of God in the human being and of God's salvific, liberating work in relation to the human being. And Barth's theology is no exception in this regard. I had the privilege of working closely with Thornton on his dissertation, "Cyborg Trans/Criptions: Gender, Disability, and the Image of God," which, when revised and published as a monograph, will make a valuable and much-needed contribution to theological and religious discourse on these issues. I have attempted to make pertinent gestures in this direction in my final revisions of the already overdue manuscript, but they are woefully inadequate and much more needs to be said and done. For starters, there should be a section on Barth's theological ethics and ableism in the last chapter. Here's hoping for a second edition!

14. See, for example: Jesus Christ "is the Word spoken from the loftiest, most luminous transcendence and likewise the Word heard in the deepest, darkest immanence . . . Thus He comes forward to *man* on behalf of *God* calling for and awakening faith, love, and hope, and to *God* on behalf of *man*, representing man, making satisfaction and interceding. Thus He attests and guarantees to man God's free grace and at the same time attests and guarantees to God man's free gratitude. Thus He establishes in His Person the justice of God vis-à-vis man and also the justice of man before God . . . in which God speaks and man hears, God gives and man receives, God commands and man obeys . . ." (Barth, "Humanity of God," 46–47).

However, while Jesus's creaturely yes is spoken and enacted for us—for all, for each and every one—it is not yet all that God desires. For God desires that this concrete creaturely yes might be taken upon the lips of all creatures, repeated in their own voice and with their own agency—to whatever extent possible—in creaturely freedom and responsibility. Consequently, Barth suggests that when we *subjectively* (with heart, mind, and body; with our whole, embodied life) say yes to what *objectively* occurs in Jesus Christ (through the Spirit)—as not only God's Yes to us, but as the creaturely yes back to God (and in God, to the neighbor, the last, first) for which we were made and for which creation was brought into and is sustained in existence—*we* might then find the freedom to speak and live that yes in our own voices and our own bodies, to repeat that yes in whatever weak, frail, broken, equivocal, and impermanent echo we can muster in our own particular circumstances.

The Exclusionary Constriction of Particularity: What We Cannot Say

If we are the human creatures God created us to be only in what *occurs* in the concrete, eternal-historical *event* that is God only and wholly for us—*and us for God* (and in God, for each other, the last, first)—in Jesus (through the Spirit), then there is no general essence or nature of human being rooted in the orders or structures of creation and nature and therefore knowable through whatever knowledge of those structures and orders we may be able to achieve at any given time. (As we will see in chapter 7, this becomes one of the more obvious areas of inconsistency in Barth. There are key points in his theological anthropology, in the context of his doctrine of creation, where he can be found retreating from this fundamental insight into more traditional habits of thinking, even into forms of natural theology. This is particularly true of his treatments of gender and sexuality.) We cannot understand or define human nature apart from the eternally willed and concretely actualized event that is the creaturely yes to God's Yes—and in God, to the neighbor, the last, first—that occurs in Jesus (through the Spirit).

This is another instance of the methodological consequences noted early on in this chapter. The church's theological anthropology (i.e., its doctrine of the human being) is not to be primarily grounded in either the creation narratives of Genesis nor a Christian doctrine of creation considered independently from the eternal-historical, Trinitarian will, decision, Word, and act that occurs in Jesus (through the Spirit) as the meaning of creation itself. While Barth can be seen to think with tradition in terms of at least the bare bones of Chalcedonian Christology, he departs from much of it in terms of how Christology is related to theological anthropology. For Barth, Christian theological anthropology must be rooted in the prophetic and apostolic witness to the life of Jesus, not in the biblical accounts of Adam and Eve in the garden and/or the doctrinal context of creation, where most of Christian theological tradition has rooted it throughout its various histories.

Consequently, the "*only* in Jesus Christ" means that the church must not only begin with what it knows in Jesus Christ (through the Spirit) and work backwards to its doctrine of God. It must also begin with what it knows in Jesus Christ (through the Spirit) and work backwards to its doctrine of the human being.[15] Under the constriction of the *only*, the church must begin with the particular event of human, creaturely reality that occurs in Jesus (through the Spirit) as the context, reason, and meaning of all history and reality—again, the particular is the context for the universal. Indeed, as Barth believes *all* Christian thinking, speaking, and living must begin with what we know concretely in Jesus Christ (through the Spirit), Christians and churches must work either backwards or forwards from there to *every* Christian doctrine, theological theme, or biblical testimony, making the necessary adjustments, corrections, and exegetical interpretations to whatever one finds there as received from tradition.

Here, Barth's theology is again at odds with a positive, doctrinal form of religious pluralism, as well as with non-religious philosophical, aesthetic, ethical, and cultural discourses, in being unable to affirm any natural capacity—religious or otherwise—to know and assess, diagnose and remedy, the true nature and full dimensions of human being and creaturely reality. Barth's theology excludes the possibility that who we are as human creatures might in fact be quite different from what is enacted and known in Jesus (through the Spirit). Now, as we will see more clearly in the following chapters, this is *not* to say that various religious—or non-religious—traditions are incapable of viewing the human creature and the material world in ways that resonate strongly with what is known of the creature in Jesus (through the Spirit) in an *ad hoc* way. Nor is it to deny the possibility that any variety of religious or non-religious traditions and practices may, and in fact do, witness more faithfully to who we are created and called to be in Jesus (through the Spirit) than does the church in any given context. But there is no getting around the conflictual difference between Barth and liberal and progressive theologies on the possibility for understanding the human and creaturely condition in

---

15. See, for example: We "must first look away from man in general and concentrate on the one man Jesus, and only then look back from Him to man in general" (Barth, *Dogmatics* III/2, 53).

all its paradoxical depth and complexity apart from what is eternally decided and made concretely actual in Jesus (through the Spirit).

However, as we have also seen, this conflictual difference is complicated by *what else* is excluded—by what else we *cannot say*—in the "*only* in Jesus Christ," as it relates to the reality and meaning of human, creaturely existence. We are again revisiting ground already covered: any and every creaturely no to God—with all its destructive consequences for the creature themselves, the neighbor, and creation—is excluded as the final word and meaning of the creature's historical life and eternal future.

For Barth, of course, this creaturely no is a reality, and a very serious one. It does occur, all the time. It is an expression of the destructive principalities and powers of sin that hold the creature captive. Accordingly, for Barth, the divine wrath over and judgment upon this destructive creaturely no is a reality, and a very serious one. It has occurred. It has been fully enacted and executed on the cross of Jesus (in the Spirit), where God takes and accepts the full reality of sin—of the creaturely no to God, and in this no, to the neighbor and to creation itself—into God's very life and as God's responsibility.[16] God judges sin by taking it—the creaturely no to God, together with the full scope of its destructive consequences—into God's own life, refusing to let that destructive no be the final creaturely word. The creaturely yes of Jesus (in the Spirit), in answering and meeting God's eternal Yes to the creature, blows through the bottom of hell and the power of death itself, judging and destroying the latter's capacity to finally determine the historical life and eternal future of the creature. As we have seen, for Barth, Christians and churches are forbidden to believe in the creaturely no. They can only believe in the divine Yes and corresponding creaturely yes spoken and enacted in Jesus (through the Spirit). Christians and churches are forbidden to see any creaturely no to God—yea, to see sin itself—as the last and final word upon the meaning and future of creaturely life.[17] Unfortunately, from Barth's perspective,

16. See, for example: "And because the eternal divine predestination is identical with the election of Jesus Christ, its twofold content is that God wills to lose in order that man may gain. There is a sure and certain salvation for man, and a sure and certain risk for God . . . in the election of Jesus Christ . . . God has ascribed to man the former, election, salvation and life; and to Himself He has ascribed the latter, reprobation, perdition and death . . . The risk and threat is the portion which the Son of God, i.e., God Himself, has chosen for His own" (Barth, *Dogmatics* II/2, 166–67).

17. See "The Election of the Individual," in Barth, *Dogmatics* II/2, 306–506. For example, see: "The elect . . . cannot give more credence to the limitation in which he sees both others and himself involved than to the promise by which he himself lives in spite of his godlessness. He can and must, of course, take it seriously as a participation in the unholy attempt to oppose the grace conferred on men by Jesus Christ. But he cannot

the traditional church has almost always insisted on seeing, believing in, and empowering the creaturely no and the reality of sin in just this way.

The Inclusionary Universal Embrace: What We Must Say

Here, again, we can only repeat what has been clearly implied and in some instances explicitly stated from the very beginning. For Barth, the "*only* in Jesus Christ" can only mean *all* in Jesus Christ, the last, first. In particular, all human creatures are equally human in the eternal-historical event that occurs in Jesus Christ (through the Spirit). As we all equally receive our creaturely humanity in the objectively and concretely actual eternal-historical event that occurs in Jesus's creaturely yes to God (in the Spirit), and in God, to the neighbor, the last, first, we receive the possibility of witnessing to that creaturely humanity in events of freedom, responding with our own yeses in our own voices, in our own lives, and with our own bodies, to whatever extent that is possible for any given creature.

For Barth, the gospel news about God with and for us all in Jesus (through the Spirit), the last, first, is not only about the great good news of what God has willed, said, and done for us. It is also the good news that, in the history, relation, and event that occurs in Jesus Christ (through the Spirit), our creaturely humanity has acted, as well. Our creaturely yes back to God has been spoken, lived, and enacted once for all. Creaturely human life, in all its genuine yet limited, dependent agency, has been made concretely actual according to God's eternal will and decision.

Yes, there is a very real sense that, in the face of sin, and in and through the Incarnation, God ultimately has to do both parts in this history of call and response between divine and creaturely wills, decisions, words, and actions. However, it is essential to the mystery of the Incarnation, and of the reconciliation and redemption in the face of sin accomplished in it, that God is in fact *fully human* in Jesus (through the Spirit) and so acts in and with a genuine creaturely response. Again, the one Word of *God* that is God only and wholly for us in Jesus (through the Spirit) includes (albeit mysteriously, miraculously) a genuine, *creaturely* word and action that is only and wholly

---

reckon with any final validity or power of this opposition, or success of this attempt, even on the part of his neighbour. As he believes that the supremacy of the elect Jesus Christ in face of the rejected is true for himself, he must and will believe that it is true for the other . . . *His defiance of others will mean that he does not grant them any final competence to play the role of the rejected . . . In light of the Gospel . . . the rejected . . . is a shadow which yields and dissolves and dissipates, being clearly limited by God*" (Barth, *Dogmatics* II/2, 454; my emphasis).

for God, and in God, for the neighbor, the last, first. For Barth, the church is required to proclaim—it *must say*—to and for *all*, that the creaturely yes to God spoken and lived in Jesus (through the Spirit) is *their* creaturely yes. It is the actualization of their concrete, objective reconciliation to God that addresses them as *invitation* and *permission* to take up this creaturely yes with their own lips, lives, and bodies in joyful gratitude and freedom, to whatever extent that is possible for them in their concrete particularity. For Barth, the creature is addressed by invitation and permission—as divine command, yes, as we will see in the next chapters, but command as a call into true creaturely freedom and agency—as distinct from an absolute requirement *upon which the winning and securing of God's redemptive Yes to their creaturely existence precariously hangs*. Unfortunately, from Barth's perspective, the traditional church has almost always either failed or refused to speak this good word, preferring to trade in requirement and *quid pro quo*, addicted to an idolatrous possessing and policing of the mechanisms of salvation.

The Bible—*Only* in Jesus Christ

As we have seen, for Barth, the Bible is the authoritative, written human witness to the one living Word of God that is God for us in Jesus (through the Spirit). This is true of both the prophetic and the apostolic witness in Scripture, that is, of both the Hebrew Scriptures and the Christian New Testament. This means that, for Barth, Jesus Christ constitutes the sole *theological* content (i.e., for the life of *faith*) of what Christians and churches have received as our canonical Scriptures, i.e., the Bible—and so functions as the unity of both testaments—*if and when* it is read by the church as witness to the one Word of God and in expectation that it might *become* that Word in an event of free divine address and self-giving. God for us all in Jesus (through the Spirit), the last, first, is the one Word of God for which—and *only* for which—the church must always listen in all its reading, exegeting, interpreting, preaching, and hearing of the Bible, no matter which passage or page is being read, including passages and pages in the Hebrew Scriptures. The Hebrew Scriptures, then, when read by the church in this way and for this hearing, are believed to find their full meaning in the apostolic witness to Jesus—*when the living reality of Jesus, as God for us all, the last first, speaks through it (in the Spirit)*.

There is no getting around the fact that this is a supersessionist reading of the Hebrew Scriptures. It is a supersessionist reading that is structured and determined by a supersessionist theological vision more generally. Barth is thinking *with* the supersessionist grain of Christian theological tradition in seeing not only the Hebrew Scriptures, but the history, reality, identity, and meaning of the people of Israel, Judaism, and the Jewish neighbor more generally, as being determined not in and by themselves and their own self-understanding and self-definition, but—as with *all* creaturely reality—only in and by that divine-human reality to which the church points when it witnesses to what it believes to be the God of Israel's one eternal will, decision, Word, and act to be God *only* in Jesus Christ—for *all*, the last, first. And this is a problem.

This is a problem because Christian supersessionism is a problem. Any and all forms of Christian supersessionism in relation to the Hebrew Scriptures, Judaism, and the Jewish neighbor are essentially and problematically related—albeit to varying degrees of complicity—to the violent, destructive history of Christian anti-Judaism and antisemitism that has been a central and consistent feature of church history from the beginning.[18] I have attempted, in other work, to show the complexity of the structures and realities of Christian supersessionism, both in general and in Barth's theology in particular.[19] I will not repeat that work here. I will simply propose that, as in all things—as I trust is becoming clear for the reader by this point—Barth's theology is a very specific form of the problem that can also be seen to entail (a) its own self-critical judgment and critique of that problem, especially as regards the material violence of supersessionist Christian history, and (b) its own resources for inhabiting the (what I argue are inescapable) risks of Christian supersessionism *otherwise*, not only *without weapons* but *with* an unequivocal commitment to the material well-being and flourishing of the Jewish neighbor, in the company of all neighbors.[20]

The questions that remain open and that need to be continually pursued: (a) Is it possible for liberal, progressive, and liberationist Christian theologies to escape their own forms of supersessionism and anti-Judaism? (I argue it is not.) (b) To what extent is Barth's particular form of supersessionism complicated and displaced by his intractable affirmation of the history of Israel as that through which the God known in Jesus Christ blesses and redeems *both* Israel *and* the nations (i.e., "salvation is from the Jews" [John 4:22])? (c) In what ways and to what extent does the *content* of Barth's

18. For critical Christian engagements with this history, see Reuther, *Faith and Fratricide*; Eckardt, *Elder and Younger Brothers*; Littell, *Crucifixion of the Jews*.

19. For another thorough treatment of the issues of supersessionism and anti-Judaism in Barth, see Sonderegger, *Born a Jew*.

20. I take the "without weapons" language from Gary Dorrien's book on Barth: Dorrien, *Theology without Weapons*. I use this phrase again in a subheading in the following chapter.

theological supersessionism—i.e., the theological content of his "*only* in Jesus Christ"—*prevent* the divine wrath, judgment, and rejection witnessed to in Scripture from being believed or acted on by Christians and churches as the last word to the Jewish neighbor; and to what extent does it call Christians and churches to *commit themselves*—unequivocally and irrevocably—to the historical and material well-being and flourishing of the Jewish neighbor, as closest among creaturely neighbors? (d) How does that same theological content prevent Christian acknowledgment of the closeness of the Jewish neighbor from being translated into a diminishment and marginalization of Christian commitment to all other creaturely neighbors as equally affirmed and embraced in and by the one Word of God that is God for us *all* in Jesus (through the Spirit), the last, first?

QUESTIONS

1. Why could one say that *from God*, while the primary movement and direction of Christian theological thinking and speaking, is nevertheless not enough, for Barth? That is, why is it not sufficient to the goodness of the gospel news, as he understands it? Put differently, why could one argue that it would be more faithful to Barth's theology to have put chapter 5 (*only* in Jesus Christ) before chapter 4 (*from God*)?

2. How does the challenge of Barth's "*only* in Jesus Christ" to traditional theological understandings of and approaches to natural and special revelation relate to your own theology and/or theological context? Is it a challenge to be resisted or welcomed as an invitation to new understanding? Why? How is the meaning of long-cited biblical references to natural revelation, such as "the heavens declare the glory of God" (Ps 19:1 KJV), determined by Barth's approach?

3. What does it mean that Barth's "*only* in Jesus Christ" is not just an *epistemological* limit, *for us*—i.e., saying that we can only *know* God in and through Jesus Christ (and the Spirit)—but is also and even primarily a limit of *God's* own reality and being—i.e., that *God* chooses to only *be* God in and through Jesus Christ (and the Spirit)? How is this constriction of the "only" a *good* thing, for Barth? That is, how is it essential to the goodness of the gospel; what *bad* stuff gets excluded? Do *you* think it is a good thing? Why or why not?

4. Why does Barth want to ground our theological anthropology (i.e., our theological knowledge of the human being) in Jesus Christ rather than

in Adam and Eve? What implications does this have for how you understand human nature? For how you read the Bible, particularly the creation narratives?

PART 3

THE ETHICS OF BARTH'S THEOLOGY

"How Should We Then Live?"

6

WE DO STUFF TOO

Human Agency, Freedom, and Action

DIVINE CALL AND CREATURELY RESPONSE

IT CAN OFTEN SEEM like Barth is so focused on the priority, primacy, sovereignty, and sufficiency of who God is and what God does that there is not much, if anything, left for the creature to do. It seems that God does everything and we do nothing; that God alone acts, and we only receive, passively and inertly; that God alone is capable and we are quite radically and specifically incapable of anything. This charge is frequently made against Barth's theology from both theological conservatives on the right and theological progressives on the left.

Barth would no doubt say that it only *seems* like that is the case for both conservatives and progressives because they both, each in their own way, want the human creature to be more at the center of the story and so have more power and control in determining the story, including power and control to determine both God's and the neighbor's story. He would argue, correspondingly, that it is this desire for power and control—and its accompanying refusal to inhabit the creaturely sphere in a way appropriate to the creature, in radical and thankful embrace of creaturely limitation in dependence upon God and God's gracious will and action—that is the true problem.

For our part, regardless of whether Barth leaves *enough* room or not, we can clearly say that he does in fact leave room for creaturely agency and action. It simply is not the case that Barth's theology eviscerates or erases the sphere of genuine creaturely agency, action, freedom, responsibility, and ethics. Indeed, we have already seen that, for Barth, everything God wills, does, and says is for the sake of a creaturely response. God's Yes to the creature is precisely for the sake of a free creaturely yes back to God (and in God, to and for the neighbor, the last, first). Even more radically, we have seen that the reality, action, and event of the Word of God itself is always also an historical, material, creaturely reality, word, and action. It always *includes* a creaturely reality, word, and action: primarily, in the fully human person of Jesus and Jesus's creaturely yes to God's Yes; secondarily, in the radically questionable, frail—yea, sinful—creaturely words and actions of witness and testimony through which the Word of God always comes to us and finds us, *if and when* God chooses.[1]

Consequently, while we can and should argue whether or not Barth leaves *enough* room or not for creaturely agency, freedom, and action—and whether or not it is the right *kind* of agency, freedom, and action: agential enough, free enough, self-determining (i.e., sovereign) enough—Barth cannot be interpreted fairly as leaving *no* room for genuine creaturely action. This is obvious in Barth's own life, in the way he inhabited his own Christian faith and lived out his theology in a socially and politically engaged way (to the extent that he was consistent in doing so, which was not always). But it is also evident in the structure of his multi-volume *Church Dogmatics*. Every volume of *Church Dogmatics* but the first, which is focused on the Word of God itself, concludes with a part-volume on ethics, focusing on what the eternal Word of God that is God for us in Jesus (through the Spirit), the last, first, means for concrete creaturely life: us for God, and in God, for each other, the last, first. Each volume ends by addressing the Word of God as divine call for creaturely response, for a creaturely decision, word, and action in and for a particular time and place.

This means that, for Barth, the church's work of theology can never avoid, dismiss, or otherwise divorce itself from the question of ethics, of faithful and responsible individual and communal, social and political action in and for the neighbor and the world. The theologian—or the person of faith, more generally—can never defer or relegate ethics to someone else as a task separate from and secondary to the proper work of theology. The church's theological thinking and speaking and acting always includes ethics, is always about ethical thinking and speaking and acting in an essential

---

1. For in depth work on Barth's ethics, see Migliore, *Commanding Grace*; Biggar, *Hastening That Waits*.

way. This departs from the habit of much traditional theology, in both the church and the academy, of regulating ethics to a secondary status in relation to dogmatic, systematic, or doctrinal theology, the work of presumedly lesser mortals in presumedly secondary disciplines.

This also means that Barth sees Christian ethics as fundamentally a *theological* task. It is fundamentally and organically internal to the work of theology. And this can be seen as less than good news for many Christian ethicists, particularly more progressive ethicists on the left. First of all, as a general rule, traditional theologians have proved they cannot be trusted to give ethics the serious attention it deserves, and Barth's emphasis on the priority, primacy, sovereignty, and sufficiency of divine will and action is not seen as great evidence that he can or does behave differently in any significant way. Secondly, from a progressive theological as well as ethical point of view, Barth's methodological and theological prioritizing of God and God's act of redeeming and reconciling self-revelation in relation to the creature, together with the corresponding priority of the God-creature relation over the creature-creature relation as the latter's ground, condition, context, and criteria, is in itself an inherent ethical problem. From a progressive point of view (as I understand it; insufficiently, no doubt), this cannot but distort the ethical vision and discernment of ethical responsibility; it cannot but result in bad ethics; that is, be harmful to the creature and to the creaturely neighbor.

Finally, it also means that in what follows, as we now turn to look more specifically at what Barth says about the stuff *we* do, everything that Barth says in this connection is—or at least *should* be—grounded in what we have seen Barth saying and doing in the previous chapters: creaturely agency and action, saying and doing, is fundamentally made possible by, is a response to, and so is also fundamentally determined by God's agency and action, saying and doing. What follows should be so grounded *if*, that is, I am being consistent in my interpretation of Barth, and Barth himself is being consistent with the method and content of his own theology. As we will see, the latter is not always the case. Whether the former is always—or ever—the case will be for the reader to decide.

We will look at what Barth says about the stuff we do—creaturely agency, freedom, and action—in terms of three primary dimensions: the *direction* of human agency and action; the *nature* of human agency and action; the *content* of human agency and action.

PART 3: *The Ethics of Barth's Theology*

THE DIRECTION OF HUMAN AGENCY AND ACTION

We need only note two things about the direction of creaturely response to divine willing, acting, and speaking in Barth's theology. First, the agency and action of human response moves in two primary directions: back to God, and in God, to and for the creaturely neighbor. Second, these two directions are strictly ordered, the former as the foundation, context, content, and criteria of and for the latter.

Back to God

For Barth, human agency and action is not only a response to God's initiating action in the sense of being grounded in and made possible by that divine action. It is also a response specifically directed back to God. This is because, as we have seen, God's will, decision, act, and speech to and for the creature is not simply for the sake of creaturely response—and so of creaturely agency, freedom, and action—in a general, abstract sense. It is for a very specific, concrete kind of creaturely agency, freedom, and action: the agency, freedom, and action of *personal relation*. God wants to be in a very particular kind of relation with the human creature, a covenantal relation of personal freedom for love and responsibility in fellowship and communion. And it is for *this* kind of relation that God acts to and for the creature. Indeed, it is for this kind of relation that God creates in the first place.

To and for the Neighbor

There are several interrelated reasons why, for Barth, the response of creaturely agency and action called forth by divine speaking and acting is not only directed back to God, but also, secondarily, is directed to the creaturely neighbor. For one thing, the God who is *for us*, who speaks to and acts for us, who calls us into relationship, is the God who is for *all*, and so always *for the neighbor*, each and every one, in all their particularity and difference, the last, first. When we turn to God with our whole lives, with all our capacities (such as they are), intentions, and gifts, we are redirected to the neighbor, because God has already given Godself to and for the neighbor as well, the last, first. We cannot have God without the neighbor, for God has determined from all eternity not to be God without the neighbor.[2]

    2. I take the language used here from the book by Wesley Ariarajah: Ariarajah, *Not without My Neighbour*. I do this to illustrate how Barth's version of Christian theology contradicts and cannot be contained within the category created for traditional theology

Again, the God Barth believes to be for us in Jesus (through the Spirit) is for us *all*. While there is an intractable individual dimension to our existence, for Barth, we are not human beings in isolation, as separate, autonomous entities. We are only human creatures in relation to other human creatures (and we may want to say louder than Barth does: with all creatures and creation itself). In Barth's words, we are always and only human beings in "fellow-humanity," as human "being-with."³

Relatedly, in being called into concrete relationship with God, we are called as partners—albeit, yes, subordinate partners—to take up "the *causa Dei* [God's cause] in the world."⁴ For God has a cause in the world. In the Trinitarian event and history that is God for us all in Jesus (through the Spirit), the last, first, God has staked God's own life in and for the world. The creaturely world belongs to God and is loved by God and God will not see it or its creatures diminished, distorted, or destroyed—particularly those who are

---

by most liberal and progressive theologians. Ariarajah argues that Christians must give up the traditional confession that God saves only in Jesus if they are to be rightly and lovingly in solidarity with the neighbor. Such solidarity means refusing any view of salvation that does not include all neighbors. However, Barth's view of the universal and objective nature of God's salvific work that he believes occurs "*only* in Jesus Christ" does not exclude the neighbor. To the contrary, it is precisely the *only* that guarantees that no neighbor is left out or left behind. For Barth, to say "*only* in Jesus Christ" is to say nothing other than "not without my neighbor."

3. See, for example, "Man in His Determination as the Covenant-Partner of God," in Barth, *Dogmatics* III/2, 203–324. See also: "His [the human being's] ordination to be in covenant relation with God has its counterpart in the fact that his humanity, the special mode of his being, is by nature and essence a being in fellow-humanity . . . [God] wills that man's being should fulfil itself in the encounter, the relationship, the togetherness of I and Thou . . . [God] calls him to freedom in fellowship, i.e., to freedom in fellowship with others" (Barth, *Dogmatics* III/4, 116–17). Barth identifies the natural and so central form of human being-with as the fellowship between men and women. This is the source of his problematic polemic against same-sex relationships. We address this in the next chapter. Barth also uses "being with" to designate the original and final unity of the theological (and for Barth, mutually implicating and ultimately interchangeable) categories, "elected" and "rejected," when seen in the one Jesus Christ (through the Spirit). See, for example: "What other kind of reality can the elect predicate of the rejected in the form of his neighbor than the peculiar reality of this 'being-with'? In answering the question of the determination of the rejected, it is crucial that no other existence should be ascribed to the rejected than this improper and dependent 'beingwith'; that no other existence should be conceded than existence in the relationship to the elect (to Jesus Christ and to the man elected in Him)" (Barth, *Dogmatics* II/2, 453).

4. See, for example: "God wants man to be His creature. Furthermore, He wants him to be His partner. There is a *causa Dei* in the world . . . He wants man to administer and to receive justice rather than to inflict and to suffer injustice . . . He wants man to live and not to die" (Barth, "Gift of Freedom," 80–81).

last and least in the eyes of the worldly powers. For Barth, then, the life lived in intentional response to this God—what, for Barth, is the life of faith—is therefore a life of taking a stand in the world, as *God's* world, for God's *cause* in the world, for God's will for the world, for God's love of the world. This is a life of definite, concrete decision and action—a life of saying very definite *yeses* and very definite *nos* in very definite contexts to the competing options and alternatives on the ground, as it were, concerning the proper ordering and living of creaturely life—*the last, first!*—which is always our creaturely life *together*. And for Barth, our creaturely life together is always an historical, social, political, economic—i.e., *material*—life. Consequently, the life lived in intentional response to God's will, decision, Word, and action is always a creaturely life of historical, social, political, economic decision and action, taking up God's cause in the world, attempting to witness to what our creaturely life together looks like when God's will is done on earth as in heaven.

The last thing to say in this connection is simply to reiterate that the creaturely response to divine will and action that is directed toward the neighbor is grounded in and determined by—indeed, is *directed* by—the theologically prior and primary creaturely response directed back to God. It is in responding to *God* with and in our creaturely agency and action, speaking and doing, freedom and responsibility, that we are directed to act *to and for the creaturely neighbor* (and for creation itself), the last, first. For Barth, the God-relation is always the ground, possibility, context, content, and criteria of and for the creature-creature relation; and it is from this strict order and priority that the church's theological thinking about these two relations must always receive its own direction.

THE NATURE OF HUMAN AGENCY AND ACTION

Barth understands the nature of human creaturely response to God's self-giving, reconciling Word and action to be that of *free obedience*. Now, this is a very counterintuitive notion, and we should probably resign ourselves to the fact that it will likely remain so, at least for many of us, at least to some degree. After thirty-five years of reading and thinking with Barth, it still sounds and feels wrong to me every time I hear it. However, I am convinced (at least for now) that Barth's thinking here has its own viable, albeit dialectical, theological logic. In the next few pages, I will do my best to name and briefly explicate the key issues that Barth's notion of free obedience puts into play.

Let's start with *obedience*. For Barth, the one eternal Word of God that is God wholly, unequivocally, and irrevocably for us all in Jesus (through the

Spirit), the last, first, is not only a radical, liberating, and reconciling word and work of grace to and for the creature. It also—precisely *as* this word and work of grace—enacts a *claim* upon the creature: I am your God and you are my people. We do not belong to ourselves. We belong to God; and not in a general, abstract way, but in a very definite, concrete way, for the sake of a very definite, concrete form of personal relation of love and responsibility. This definite, concrete kind of relation looks like something in particular when enfleshed in the material conditions of creaturely life together. It looks like something in particular that can be distinguished from other forms of relation. Being *for* the neighbor, the last, first, in our material—i.e., social, political, economic—lives together can be distinguished from being *against* the neighbor, especially those neighbors who are last and least in the eyes of the world. More specifically, life, love, equality, mutuality, reciprocity, interdependence, and justice in our embodied, material lives together can be distinguished from death, hate, hierarchy, domination, isolation, and oppression in the realm of that same embodied materiality.

For Barth, then, the one Word of God that is God for us all in Jesus (through the Spirit), the last, first, is also the divine command.[5] The gospel of radical grace entails within it the law of God, the communication of God's concrete will for creaturely life together: be for God, and in God, be for each other, the last, first! Barth calls this the imperative that is entailed within the indicative of the Word and act of God that is Jesus Christ (in the Spirit).[6] The indicative tells us who we are by virtue of what God has willed and done for us in the Trinitarian history of creation, reconciliation, and redemption: we are created, reconciled, and redeemed to be for God, and in God, for each other, the last, first. The divine command, as the imperative entailed in the indicative, simply calls us *to be and live out who we are* as determined by the Trinitarian history and reality that is God for us in Jesus (through the Spirit): be, live, and act who and as you have been created, reconciled, and redeemed to be, live, and act! In this way, as we have seen, the divine command,

---

5. See, for example: "The Word of God applies to us as no human word as such can do . . because this Word is the Word of our Creator, of the One who encompasses our existence and the end of our existence . . . He who makes Himself heard here is the One to whom we belong" (Barth, *Dogmatics* I/1, 141); "We must be constantly aware of this point as we consider all the divine work grounded upon the grace of God and the divine election of grace. There is no grace without the lordship and claim of grace. There is no dogmatics which is not also and necessarily ethics" (Barth, *Dogmatics* II/2, 12). See especially, "The Command of God," in Barth, *Dogmatics* II/2, 509–781. See, for example: "As the grace of God is actualized and revealed, He claims men. His love commands" (Barth, *Dogmatics* II/2, 566).

6. See, for example, Barth, "Christian Ethics," 114.

for Barth, is also invitation and permission. The call to obedience *from this particular God in their concrete Word and act to and for us*, as distinct from obedience as an abstract concept (this kind of distinction must *always* be made if we are not to lose sight of Barth's meaning)—this call to obedience is not an imposed constriction keeping us from inhabiting the creaturely good in all its fullness; it is a call *into* the creaturely good in all its fullness. Barth's view of obedience, then, in its radical concreteness, can often run against the grain of theological, philosophical, and ethical habits of thinking about obedience for many of us.

Now, for the *real* mind-bending part: *free* obedience. The first thing to say is that, similar to Barth's distinctive view of obedience in the context of the gospel, what Barth means by creaturely *freedom* challenges many of our default assumptions, particularly in the West. Again, for Barth, everything about the human creature, and about creation itself, can only be rightly approached and understood, theologically speaking, as always already in response to and so as determined by prior, initiating, creating, reconciling, and redeeming divine will, decision, Word, and action directed to and for the creature. Consequently, for Barth, there is no creaturely freedom existing naturally in some general, abstract way that is the property and possession of the human creature, prior to or apart from the free, initiating divine Word and action that is God for us all in Jesus (through the Spirit), the last, first.

Human freedom is only a possibility, and only becomes actual, in and as response to divine Word and action that is also the divine command, the imperative in the indicative: be who you are created, reconciled, and redeemed to be! That is to say, we can only act freely—enact, enflesh, and inhabit genuine creaturely freedom—in and as response to the Word of God, which is to say, in obedience to the divine command, in obedience to the imperative in the indicative. For Barth, freedom is not something we *have*. It is not a capacity or property we possess; nor is it a static or fixed state we are *in*. It is something we *do*—and something we are *enabled* to do only as response to the divine claim and command.

This is what feels so weird. When we think of obedience, we tend to think of doing what we are told, following the rules, or obeying an order. When we think of freedom, we are likely to think of what can feel to us as just the opposite. We are likely to think of doing what we want, to think of the freedom to choose to do what we want, to choose what we want to do. This is especially true for those of us who have been formed in modern, Western contexts determined by neoliberal individualism, capitalism, consumerism, and the free market. We generally do not think of (a) doing what we're told, following the rules/obeying orders, and (b) being free to do what we want, being free to choose, as being the same thing. In fact, we experience them as *opposite* things. To obey, to do what you're told, is precisely *not* to be free to do what you want, to choose what you want to do. To be called to obedience is experienced as an impingement upon or violation of our freedom, not its possibility and actuality.

Barth, however, does not believe genuine freedom is simply being able to do what we want; he does not think it is simply having freedom of choice. And this is because, for Barth, to think of freedom in this way is to think of it in a general, abstract way, which is to say, apart from (a) the concrete Word of God that makes a claim upon our lives and upon all of life—as divine command—*and* (b) the reality of sin, in the grip of which the Word of God *cum* divine command always finds us.

For Barth, sin is resistance to God's Yes to and for the creature and creation. On one level, it is what human creatures do in and with our no to God's Yes that always finds a corresponding, destructive echo in a no to the creaturely neighbor. But on a more fundamental level, sin is a mysterious power in whose grip we always already *are*. It is always already *happening to* us, we are in the midst of it, comprehended by it, held captive by it. We live *in* it. And to the extent that we are always already in the captive grip of sin, we are always already in *un*freedom. The freedom to do what we want or to exercise an abstract freedom of choice, when inhabited either apart from or in resistance to God's Yes to and for the creature and creation, is simply an enactment of our lack of genuine freedom; it is an enactment of our captivity.

Barth understands genuine creaturely freedom as freedom *for God*, and in God, *for the neighbor*, the last, first, precisely as concrete response to God's being *for us*. This creaturely freedom is enacted in definite, concrete will, decision, and action in these definite, concrete relationships as determined by the Yes of God's one eternal Word and act for the creature and creation that is God for us in Jesus (through the Spirit), the last, first. It is not abstract freedom of choice. And this is what is so difficult to get our heads around: genuine creaturely freedom is not the freedom of choice, *at least not as we usually think of it*, but the freedom *of obedience*. Though again (and again and again and again), this is not *abstract* obedience, not obedience in the general sense. It is the very specific obedience to the concrete divine claim and command of God's Yes to and for the creature: be who you are in God's Yes to and for you and the neighbor, the last, first! Yes, we have a form of abstract, arbitrary freedom of choice, to a certain extent: I can turn left or right when I walk out my front door. But seen theologically, at least for Barth, that is not necessarily the fullness of genuine creaturely freedom. Whether it is genuine creaturely freedom or not depends on the concrete context in and for which the divine command is heard.

Again, for Barth, the divine claim and command has particular, concrete content, but that content is not a predetermined list of tasks or obligations or behaviors.[7] Consequently, creaturely obedience to the divine command is not undertaken and fulfilled either in the rote, thoughtless implementation of a predetermined program, agenda, or checklist, or in a coerced, strictly dictated and policed fulfillment of a command. The divine command's concrete content is that which occurs between God and the creature in Jesus Christ (through the Spirit). In this concrete act and event, the creature is determined to be for God, in and for a covenant relation of fellowship and communion. And in the context of this primary relation, the creature is also determined to be for the neighbor, the last, first (and, again, we might want to say, louder than Barth does: for all of creation). This latter determination is to be enacted and inhabited in definite, concrete forms of creaturely fellowship and communion, of love, justice, and mutual blessing, in all the materiality—i.e., the historical, social, cultural, political, economic dimensions—of creaturely life together. However, precisely what these concrete forms of creaturely relation are to look like, what shape they are to take or to be given in any particular context, at any given time and place—any given *here and now*—is not necessarily strictly dictated by the divine claim and command.

Be for God, and in God, for the neighbor, the last, first! If obedience to this command in and for a particular context can only be enacted by turning in one direction and not the other when I walk out my front door, in choosing *between* turning left or right—for example, turning left and *not* right—then the abstract freedom of choice to turn either left or right is not an expression of genuine creaturely freedom. Only the choice to turn in the direction that corresponds to the divine command—the last, first!—(in this example, turning left and *not* right) can be an enactment of genuine creaturely freedom. However, if obedience to this divine command can be enacted by turning

7. See, for example: "The question of good and evil is never answered by man's pointing to the authoritative Word of God in terms of a set of rules. It is never discovered by man or imposed on the self and others as a code of good and evil actions, a sort of yardstick of what is good and evil. Holy Scripture defies being forced into a set of rules; it is a mistake to use it as such . . . To offer ethical norms to a man in this predicament [hearing the divine imperative/command in the divine indicative of grace in and for a particular, concrete "here and now"] is to hold out a stone instead of bread" (Barth, "Gift of Freedom," 85); "What is the significance of the Bible for Christian ethics? The answer to this is *not* that the Bible is some sort of law book for Christian ethics" (Barth, "Christian Ethics," 110; my emphasis).

either left *or* right—again, *in and for a particular context*—then the choice to turn left or right *can* be an enactment of genuine creaturely freedom, an expression of responsible creaturely creativity and discernment. For example, perhaps the context is such that both the way to the left and to the right offer robust, albeit different, resources for fulfilling the divine command in and for that context.

The divine command calls on all of the creature's individual and communal dimensions, orders, capacities, gifts, and possibilities (whatever those happen to entail and whatever state they happen to be in) to be taken up in a free, intentional, and decisive act of being for God and neighbor (again, according to whatever the creature is capable of, or to whatever creaturely capacity and ability might mean, in any given context), of saying yes back to God, and in God, to the neighbor, the last, first: our reason and our curiosity, such as they are; our creativity and our imagination, such as they are; our wildest dreams, visions, and aspirations, such as they are; that is, our whole embodied selves, individual and communal, such as they are. The divine claim and command calls us to bring forth all we are in responsible and faithful discernment, assessment, decision, creativity, and imagination, such as we are able, to choose between and/or to create new concrete forms of creaturely life together that are obedient to the divine command, to the divine Yes to and for the creature and creation.

Think of our example of turning left or right, above, in light of God's commission to Adam and Eve to name the other animals. For Barth, genuine creaturely freedom in this story is enacted in the human animal's obedient act of naming the other animals; it would *not* be enacted as the "freedom of choice" *to obey or not obey* this divine commission. However, in enacting creaturely freedom in this concrete act of obedience, Adam and Eve are called and enabled to exercise a certain "freedom of choice" in *how* they obey the divine commission, that is, in what they actually choose to name the other animals. In this respect, we can say that God wanted to see what the human animals would come up with. Similarly, as long as the decision to turn left or right is not a decision *whether to obey or not to obey* the divine command to be for the neighbor, the last, first, but is a decision about *how to obey* that command, a decision between different possible ways to obey that command, then the decision to turn left or right in obedient fulfillment of that command *can* be an enactment of genuine creaturely freedom, an expression of responsible creaturely creativity and discernment, assessment and imagination: God wants to see what the human animal will come up with.

THE CONTENT OF HUMAN AGENCY AND ACTION

If we are thinking with Barth, consideration of the concrete content of the creaturely yes responding to God's Yes to and for the creature must follow the order and priority of the two directions of this creaturely response: back to God, and in God, to and for the neighbor. As we have seen, the response back to God takes priority for Barth as the ground and context determining the response that is directed to and for the neighbor.

Creaturely Response Directed Back to God: Gratitude

For Barth, the creaturely response directed back to God's Word and action can appear to have as simple and singular a content as Barth's understanding of the Word of God itself. Both early and late in his *Church Dogmatics*, Barth sums up the creaturely response to the one Word that is God for us in Jesus (through the Spirit) with another single word: gratitude. As we have seen, the entire content of God's one eternal will, decision, Word, and act to and for the creature in the Trinitarian reality, person, history, and relation that is God for us in Jesus (through the Spirit) is the Yes of grace, and so of love, mercy, reconciliation, and liberation. Correspondingly, the beginning, end, and entire content of the creature's yes back to God is the yes of gratitude. In a very real sense, for Barth, there is nothing else for the creature to say.[8]

The forcefulness of Barth's language in making this point can at times be alarming from the ethical point of view. On numerous occasions, Barth can be found saying quite clearly that gratitude is the *only* response of the creature to God's will, Word, and act to and for the world.[9] Without context, this can

---

8. Barth also names keeping the Sabbath, confession (bearing witness), and prayer as specific actions of creaturely activity that are directed to God. See Barth, *Dogmatics* III/4, 47–115. I focus on gratitude both because of the limits of space and because of the *only and always* language Barth uses in relation to it. While none of the other three are accompanied by this *only and always* language in the same way, prayer is parenthetically acknowledged to have a certain form of this dimension: "Like confession, prayer is a particular and concrete action. It is certainly true that it *may and must be the perennial undertone, basis and support accompanying and upholding all other human actions* . . . But it is even more true . . . that this constant state may and must continually take concrete form in individual moments and specific actions" (Barth, *Dogmatics* III/4, 88–89; my emphasis). Also, confession/bearing witness is simultaneously a creature-directed action, as proclamation, as addressed in the following.

9. See, for example: "[T]he covenant of grace . . . engages man as the partner of God only, but actually and necessarily, to gratitude . . . For the other partner . . . to whom God turns in this grace, the *only* proper thing, but the thing which is unconditionally and inescapably demanded, is that he should be thankful. How can anything more or different

appear to be saying that the creature is entirely relieved of—indeed, prevented from—any action in the realm of their historical, material life that bears upon the neighbor and the historical world shared with the neighbor. Concrete works of love and justice, for example, seem to be completely eclipsed in Barth's theological vision here. And if that is really what is going on, we are right to be alarmed. However, I don't believe that is really what is going on.

One can only come to the conclusion that this is what Barth really means by ignoring massive amounts of his work and repeated articulations of his theological vision. Barth does indeed make these strong statements. But I believe that when read in context, they are intended to express two key points, neither of which either explicitly or implicitly excludes action to and for the neighbor. The first point is to emphasize what Barth assumes to be the incomparable magnitude and wholly uncompromised nature of the goodness of the gospel news. There is truly nothing to fear in or from God, and if not in or from God, then certainly not from any other quarter. Barth never tires of trying to communicate the extent to which, if we ever truly glimpsed the full goodness of the news, the radical depth and breadth of grace—of what it means that God is wholly, unqualifiedly, and irrevocably for us concretely in Jesus (through the Spirit)—we would simply never stop jumping for joy. This is what the *only* is meant to signify when Barth says the creaturely response to the Word of God that is also the divine command is properly gratitude and only gratitude.

Secondly, then, the meaning of jumping for joy, here, is properly understood not as a singular activity that excludes all other activities, such that if and when I'm jumping for joy I would have a very hard time sleeping, feeding the baby, taking my elderly parent to the doctor, working to guarantee a living wage for myself and my neighbors, and fighting to ensure that no communities are targeted for harm by structures of racism, sexism, heteronormativity, and homophobia. It is clear that all of these latter activities are essential to the health, wholeness, and goodness of our material creaturely life together that God is *for*—and calls us *to*—in Jesus (through the Spirit) in the first place. Responding to God's Yes in a way that would diminish and endanger the very

---

be asked of man? . . . Radically and basically all sin is simply ingratitude—man's refusal of *the one but necessary thing which is proper to and is required of him*" (Barth, *Dogmatics* III/4, 41; my emphasis); "That activity of man is good, in the Christian sense, in which man acknowledges that he stands in need of this divine mercy; yet that he is not only in need of it, but also shares in it. To say it briefly: That action of man is good in which man is thankful for God's grace. *Nothing else? No, nothing else.* For everything else which might be called good, faith, love, hope, every thankful good virtue and duty, is contained in this one: that man be thankful for God's grace" (Barth, "Christian Ethics," 109; my emphasis).

creaturely life that God's Yes establishes and redeems would certainly not be free obedience to the divine command entailed and heard in that Yes. Rather, jumping for joy—i.e., for Barth, gratitude; and across various contexts, thanks, joy, praise—is best taken as the attitude, orientation, disposition, or mode of being with which *all* creaturely agency and action, saying and doing, as response to the divine Yes, is undertaken and by which it is marked and determined.

I think this is true for Barth even—and perhaps most especially—in the struggle and conflict of historical life; for example, in the righteous anger at and the fight against injustice. As fundamental, underlying orientations and dispositions, gratitude and joy are not diametrically opposable to struggle and conflict, to mourning and righteous anger. They are the ground upon which struggle, conflict, mourning, and righteous anger are taken up and inhabited as part of the agency and action of faith in certain concrete contexts. But as such, they do mark a certain limit to struggle, conflict, mourning, and righteous anger, marking the boundary that keeps righteous anger, for example, *righteous*; that keeps these inevitable dimensions of historical, material, creaturely life from becoming grounds and ends in themselves, from spilling over into and being ruled by resentment, bitterness, hate, revenge—all of which, given the often overwhelming realities of injustice and oppression, are all too understandable and even compelling responses.

Consequently, gratitude and joy are best understood in Barth's distinctively theological uses of these terms as not primarily referring to particular emotions or feelings (though our emotions and feelings are by no means excluded), but to fundamental ways or modes of being in the world, of inhabiting one's creaturely agency and action as the response of free obedience to God's will, Word, and action.

Creaturely Response Directed to the Neighbor: Proclamation and Ethics

I believe Barth's view of the creaturely direction of human response to divine will, Word, and action falls into two general categories: proclamation and ethics.

Proclamation as Witness and Testimony without Weapons

For Barth, proclamation is a particular, divinely commissioned task of the church explicitly directed toward the creaturely neighbor, both inside and outside the church, wherein the church attempts the impossible: to repeat the eternal-historical Word of God that is God for us all in Jesus (through the Spirit), the last, first, in and with its own limited, questionable, broken, and sinful creaturely words, to and for whatever concrete time and place in which it happens to find itself. For Barth, this attempt of the humanly impossible can only be understood as the church's *intended* proclamation.[10] Like the Scripture it must always read, hear, and exegete, church proclamation, in and of itself, is always and only fully human witness and testimony. But it is to be undertaken with the *intention* that it might not only witness to, but also—again, like Scripture—*become* that Word of God itself to the creaturely neighbor: "Thus saith the Lord! . . ."[11]

But beyond this creaturely *intention*—the intention of creaturely obedience to the divine command of commissioned proclamation—the church cannot go. It has no capacity to relate itself to the actual Word of God that is the living, personal Trinitarian reality, event, history, and relation of God for us in Jesus (through the Spirit), in any other way than in this frail and limited creaturely intention. In and of itself—again, like Scripture—it can always only remain fully and problematically human witness and testimony. And as such, in and of itself, it can never claim nor wield any inherent authority or power over the creaturely neighbor. It can be faithfully obedient only in transparently inhabiting its radical creaturely frailty and powerlessness. As explicitly directed to the fellow creature, intended proclamation can only be human agency and action that places the church with and alongside the neighbor, *for the neighbor*, never above or against the neighbor. It can never be delivered or

---

10. See "Talk about God and Church Proclamation" and "The Word of God Preached," in Barth, *Dogmatics* I/1, 47–70, 88–99. See, for example: "If, then, human talk about God *aims to be* proclamation, this can only mean that it wills to serve the Word of God and thus to point to its prior utterance by God Himself. *It cannot assume that it is the Word of God* . . . The human will in question can only be the will to accept a task . . . What human utterance concerning God *aims to be when it is intended as proclamation* is not grace, but service of grace or means of grace"; "*Real proclamation of the Word of God cannot be conditioned by our intention* to speak the Word of God" (Barth, *Dogmatics* I/1, 52, 53; my emphases).

11. Barth illustrates this in a striking fashion in his address to an international conference on humanism: "In fact I cannot show you the Christian proclamation as something 'here and now' at all. I cannot hand you that on a plate . . . Were this a sermon, I would have to go on to the exhortation, 'Repent and believe in the gospel.' This is, however, not a sermon . . . There remains nothing more for me to do but to consider this matter from the outside and simply make the point that it would be a question of repentance and faith, and indeed of conversion, if the Christian proclamation were to become something 'here and now' . . . And the consideration of this subject, in order for it to be a matter of 'here and now,' would of course have to begin by our praying the Lord's Prayer and celebrating the Lord's Supper together" (Barth, "Proclamation Here and Now," 11–12).

enforced with the weapons of creaturely power and control, only in creaturely vulnerability and weakness.

In all its unavoidably scandalous and offensive audacity—"This is the Word of the Lord for us today!..."—as *intended* proclamation, this creaturely action of the church knows that in and of itself it can never be more than just that: the creaturely intention of obedience. It knows that it can only *become* what Barth calls *real* proclamation *if and when* God decides to show up and speak through it in a free event of divine self-disclosure and personal address. And it has no capacity or power to anticipate, incite, instigate, create, control, or possess this event of divine freedom. It knows that here, too, it always remains true that only God can speak the Word of God; that the Word of God always and only occurs as an event of concrete address and encounter *from God*; that only God—in the free act of this event—can turn intended proclamation into *real* proclamation.

Too Much; Not Enough

Despite these strict qualifications, Barth's view of proclamation will always risk the ethical offense entailed in the scandalous audacity of even *intending* to speak the Word of God to and for the neighbor, especially from the point of view of progressive theology and ethics. What is inevitably risked is the destructive abuse of power that comes with the human claim to know, possess, and wield the Word of God, to speak *for* God, as one's own possibility and power. The church's history—at least what is seen as the normative history of the Anglo-European churches—is a history of just such damage and destruction of creaturely well-being. And it is just this history that Barth attempts to name and critique as a betrayal of the divine command that commissions *intended* proclamation—with all its strict limits and boundaries—as a form of human agency and action directed to and for the neighbor. While it would certainly be easier to avoid the risk by simply avoiding proclamation altogether, Barth believes the church cannot take this easy way out without ceasing to be the church. Instead, he lays down the gauntlet of free obedience. The divine commission by which Barth believes the church to be addressed means it is impossible to avoid the risk.

For Barth, then, *if and when* the church is obedient to the commissioned task of *intended* proclamation, it can only live by the grace of God alone, and so always in and through the constant vigil of vulnerability and humility, confession and repentance, self-critique and self-correction. Consequently, *cutting to the right*, Barth's view of proclamation is severely and relentlessly critical of conservative ecclesial and theological histories claiming to be miraculously endowed with, and so to possess and wield, the Word of God. These are histories that Barth believes are always idolatrous and destructive for the neighbor and for God's good creation. Alternatively, *cutting to the left*, Barth's view of intended proclamation traffics too intimately with what progressives see as a literalist—I think Barth would want to say *actualist*—interpretation of what church tradition has called the Word of God.[12] For a progressive theology and ethics, the concept of "the Word of God" itself remains risky even when thoroughly translated into the modern liberal category of natural symbolic expression of human religious experience (i.e., humans talking to themselves about themselves, about *our* particular religious experience of universal divine presence). So any interpretation that even hints at signifying *actual* divine speaking and acting simply runs too great a risk of enabling the church's destructive claim to *possesses and wield* actual divine speaking and acting as its own special, divinely commissioned possibility.

Barth understands the church to be called and commissioned to walk the razor's edge between these two alternatives—between fleeing from the inevitable risk of *intended* proclamation and destructively claiming the capacity for *real* proclamation. If the church is to be the church, it can only run the risk, work without a net, in the humility of free and always self-critical obedience.

---

12. The expression that something is *literally* true or that something is meant in the literal sense can have several distinct yet related meanings. Among them are two very common meanings: we can mean that something is *actually* true, has actually occurred or is actually the case, has become actual; we can also mean that something is *exactly* true, "word for word," a literal description that provides an exact copy or representation of a state or event, like we tend to think a video does. Something can be a statement of *actual* truth, of what is actually the case, what has actually happened or occurred (one meaning of literally true), without being a *literal*, exact, "word for word" description (another meaning of literally true). I suggest that, in light of these distinctions, it is more faithful to Barth's theological intention to say that he is an actualist as distinct from a literalist. The biblical witness to creation points to something that is actually true, or actually the case: God has actually created the world and is our creator; this has actually occurred and is actually the case. But the biblical witness to creation is not necessarily a literal description of the event of creation. Similarly, Chalcedonian Christology witnesses to something that can be believed as actually the case: what occurs in the life and history of Jesus (in the Spirit) is that God is fully and uniquely—and redemptively—with and for the creature in the life and history of this human creature (in the power of the Spirit). But the Chalcedonian formula is not necessarily a literal description of the metaphysical structure of God's incarnate presence in the person of Jesus of Nazareth.

Ethics without Lists, Principles, or Natural Laws

Barth's view of the content of creaturely agency and action as the response of free obedience to the divine command entailed in God's Yes to and for the creature gets a little more slippery when we turn to the realm of ethics. Barth most often defines ethics rather traditionally as the task of discerning and distinguishing between good and evil human action.[13] However, when rooted in and determined by his theological vision of the one Word of God as a free, contingent history of concrete divine will, Word, and action for the sake of a concrete creaturely response of free obedience, Barth's vision of the ethical task becomes rather untraditional.

We have already caught a glimpse of what Barth's view of creaturely agency and action, as a response of free obedience, might mean for the task of ethics. It means that the repository of pre-existing, itemized lists of good creaturely action and behavior for any concrete context is not located in all the usual places we have been taught to look for it, either within or without our religious traditions. Indeed, there is no such repository.[14] We can and should consult historical precedents and traditions as resources and guides, but in a strictly *ad hoc* fashion; we are always freed by the divine command itself to creatively employ or to set aside any and all precedents or traditions, as needed in any particular context.

As *free* creaturely obedience to the imperative entailed in the history of God's Yes to and for the creature that has occurred and does occur in Jesus Christ (through the Spirit), what counts as good creaturely action is not to be found or fulfilled by the implementation of a pre-existing list of behaviors or a pre-arranged program. The good, for Barth, is simply identical with God's own being, which is itself identical with God's will, decision, Word, and act: God only and wholly for us all in Jesus (through the Spirit), the last first, and us for God, and in God, for each other, the last, first. In terms of creaturely

---

13. See, for example: "Ethics must be understood as an attempt, scientific or otherwise, to cope with the question of good and evil in human behavior" (Barth, "Gift of Freedom," 85).

14. See especially, "The Problem of a Special Ethics," in Barth, *Dogmatics* III/4, 3–31. For example, see: "[T]his particular man . . . chooses this particular condition and possibility, deciding for it and realizing it by what he does or refrains from doing . . . until his next decision under changed conditions and in relation to new possibilities . . . In this new sphere he will face a new choice and decision" (Barth, *Dogmatics* III/4, 5–6); "[T]here is . . . no fixation of the divine command in a great or small text of ethical law; no method or technique of applying this text to the plenitude of conditions and possibilities of the activity of all men; no means of deducing good or evil in the particular instance of human conduct from the truth of this text presupposed as a universal rule and equated with the command of God" (Barth, *Dogmatics*, III/4, 9–10).

behavior and action, the good is enacted by the creature as obedient response to this divine Yes of God's good will, Word, and act in and for every particular, concrete context. And as we have seen, the freedom of this creaturely obedience calls for and involves creaturely discerning and distinguishing in which the creature is to exercise all their creativity and imagination, vision and curiosity, reason and sobriety. Again, the imperative entailed in the divine Yes calls us to free obedience—to be and live and embody who we are in and for God and for each other, the last, first, in every concrete situation—but the *freedom* of that obedience means that the divine command does not dictate a pre-existing, a-historical, supra-contextual, fixed list of action and behavior that we are to follow or implement as unreflective automatons in our enacting of that obedience.

For Barth, to undertake the task of Christian ethics as free obedience to the divine command is to always work without a net: no lists, no principles, no natural law; only historical precedents and traditions available as *ad hoc* resources and guides, to be creatively employed or rejected, depending on the Word that is heard and the needs and contours of the context in and for which it is heard. It is to be called into the true radicality of creaturely freedom and agency. This unwillingness to give fixed lists of required Christian action is simply Barth being consistent with the theological foundations of his approach to ethics.

For Barth, to give such lists in a general way, lists that exist apart from and prior to any particular situation, is precisely not to approach ethics concretely, but to approach it abstractly. For Barth, a concrete approach to ethics is rooted in hearing and responding to the event of the divine Yes in free obedience in and for a particular, concrete situation. For the one Word of God that is God for us all in Jesus (through the Spirit), the last, first, always occurs as free, contingent event in and for a particular time and place, in and for a *here and now*. And the creaturely response is correspondingly determined for that particular time and place, for a concrete here and now. What needs to be discerned and distinguished, decided and enacted in free creaturely obedience—with all the creativity, imagination, reason, experience, courage, and compassion at our disposal—is what the concrete event of the Word of God is calling us to do and say *in and for the particular time and place in which it occurs*. This cannot be done simply by implementing pre-existing lists, principles, or immutable natural laws. As Barth says in his commentary on Romans, it is not that ethical lists should or even can be avoided. We must draw up ethical lists in and for every situation. But then we must tear them up—or at least set them aside in an archive of resources to be consulted as needed in the future, but never to be blindly re-implemented in another context. We must always start again in another situation, with a new hearing of the divine command and the new creaturely response of creative discernment and decision that it calls forth. Again, God wants to see what the human animal will come up with.[15]

Finally, before we go on to consider what Barth's approach to Christian ethics might be calling us to venture in our time and place, early on in the twenty-first century, there are two points we need to be clear about. These two points constitute the tension within which Barth's theological approach to ethics lives and into which it calls Christians and churches. On one hand, Barth's view of Christian ethics is radically situational. What the Word of God means for and is calling us to in any given time and place can only be discerned in the event of that encounter in and for that time and place. As I have been noting, we do, of course, have access to what has been discerned, decided, and enacted by Christians and churches in other contexts, throughout the whole history of the church; and we also have access to histories of discernment and decision by differently religious and non-religious individuals and communities, in the contexts of their own long and storied traditions. We are, of course, to consult all these histories of discernment and decision as *ad hoc* resources and guides for the exercise of our own responsibility of free obedience. But the former can never be used as a substitute for the latter. Barth's theological approach is inherently a form of situational ethics.[16]

On the other hand, Barth is clear that being radically situational in this context is not the same thing as radical relativism. Our free creaturely obedience is always, for Barth, free *obedience*. That is, it is responsive obedience to

15. See, for example: "Those . . . who do possess this criterion [perceiving the gulf between sin and grace] are *again and again* compelled to draw up a list of sinners and righteous men and to make a catalogue of what is permitted and what is forbidden. They are bound to attempt a system of ethics. But, when this is said, it must be borne in mind that the criterion by which they are compelled to undertake this systematization also renders it no more than an attempt. The knowledge of God which is the condition of our survey compels us to distinguish clearly between sinners and righteous men; but *the human knowledge* which emerges is *at once dissolved* by the very criterion by which it was created" (Barth, *Romans*, 228; my emphases; see also, "The Great Disturbance," in Barth, *Romans*, 424–526).

16. See, for example: "[T]he power and earnestness of Christian ethics lie in its persistent asking of questions and in its steady refusal to provide answers to these questions . . . By putting an end to all absolute ethics, Christianity finally puts an end to all the triumph and sorrow that accompanies the occupation of any human eminence" (Barth, *Romans*, 466); "The possibility that from time to time God may be honoured in concrete human behavior which contradicts the commandments of the second Table must . . . be left open" (Barth, *Romans*, 451).

something concrete and in particular. There is concrete content in the divine Yes that extends a divine claim and issues in a divine command. The reader is by now sick and tired of hearing it: because God is for us all concretely in Jesus (through the Spirit), the last, first, we are to be for God, and in God, for each other, the last, first. The concreteness of God's will, decision, Word, and act that is Jesus Christ (in the Spirit) calls forth a very particular kind of personal relation of love, freedom, and justice, of communion and fellowship in covenant responsibility. As we have seen earlier, it is for *this particular concrete relation*—with both God and the neighbor, the last, first (and we may want to add, all of creation)—that we have been created and for which we have been reconciled, redeemed, and called, and for which our free creaturely obedience has been awakened. Our freedom for obedience is not a free-floating and unbound, abstract freedom of choice. It is a freedom for *this particular, concrete relation* and nothing else—for this and *nothing less*.[17]

QUESTIONS

1. How does Barth's theological understanding of freedom and obedience in the particular context of Christian ethics differ from ordinary views of freedom and obedience in modern Western consumerist cultures? Do you find Barth's approach counterintuitive to your own theological understanding? Do you experience this as an invitation or an obstacle? Why?

2. How is Barth's view of free obedience related to—informed by, grounded in—his view of the Word of God discussed in earlier chapters, as always being action, event, history, and relation (as God for us in Jesus through the Spirit)?

3. What does it mean to understand the divine command as the imperative entailed in the indicative? That is, what does the divine command mean when we hear it as the *consequence and implication of* God's act of salvation and not as the *requirement for* salvation?

4. How is creaturely creativity, imagination, discernment, and responsibility called forth by the divine command to free obedience? Identify and discuss some concrete examples of what this has looked like or might look like in your own context.

---

17. See, for example: "It is, of course, true that a quite definite manner of life is demanded in the Epistle [to the Romans]" (Barth, *Romans*, 504).

5. How is "intended proclamation," as a wholly human work of the church, distinct from "real proclamation," for Barth? How does the former *become* the latter (*if and when* it does, as Barth would say)? What is the significance of this parenthetical *if and when*?

6. How is Barth's view of Christian ethics radically situational while not being radically relativistic? Do you find this freeing or troubling? Why?

7

BARTH AND PROGRESSIVE CHRISTIAN ETHICS IN AND FOR OUR TIME AND PLACE?

CUTTING BOTH WAYS BUT *LANDING* IN A VERY PARTICULAR PLACE

FOR BARTH, ALL CHURCH proclamation and theology can only be grounded in what is given to it in the concrete Trinitarian history, relation, and event that is God for us all in Jesus (through the Spirit), the last, first. The same is true for the church's and the Christian's ethical vision and commitment; it is rooted in no other ground than what occurs and is promised in this one divine Word, event, and action. However, Barth never tires of reminding us that the content of this divine Word, event, and action is not an abstract concept or an open cipher for divine ineffability. Rather, it is a very concrete reality and event that is not only eternal but historical, wherein God has decided, willed, and acted in a very concrete and particular way, not only on behalf of the creature, but for the sake of a very concrete and particular kind of relation with the creature, a relation that determines the identity, possibility, and future (both eternally and historically) of both God and the creature in very concrete and particular ways.

In being wholly and irrevocably for us all in Jesus (through the Spirit), the last, first, God says a very definite *this* and *not that*, does a very definite *that* and *not this*. Consequently, the concrete life of the creature that is decided and enacted in the personal reality, history, relation, and event that occurs in Jesus (through the Spirit) does *not* cut both ways—i.e., to the left and to the right—*socio-politically* in exactly the same way as we have seen it cut *theologically*. Rather, it always falls on a very specific location on any available spectrum of socio-political options, and not necessarily, if ever, in "the middle."

We must be clear here. There is nothing in the essence of what God decides and enacts for the creature in Jesus (through the Spirit) that is *essentially* progressive or conservative *in itself*. For Barth, the life that the gospel calls us into is not necessarily, in itself, either progressive or conservative according to any given socio-political spectrum in any given context: both God and the creature, as decided and enacted in and by the history, relation, and event that is God for us all in Jesus (through the Spirit), the last, first, are liberated from any *necessary* relation to any particular socio-political identity in any given context. However, neither is the gospel a free-floating and contentless cipher.[1]

For Barth, then, faithfulness to the gospel *always* occupies a very specific location on any socio-political spectrum, on any given issue in any given context. Christians and churches are not free to avoid or escape taking a specific concrete socio-political stand on any given issue in any given context. Further, as we have seen, the freedom of free obedience does *not* mean that Christians or churches are always free—in the sense of an abstract freedom of choice—to take up just *any* socio-political position in a particular context. They are not free to choose a position *either* on the left *or* on the right—or in the center—of a given spectrum of opportunities on any given issue in any given context, if such a choice is a choice between either *furthering* (i.e., obedience) or *obstructing* (i.e., disobedience) God's concrete cause in the world.[2] For Barth, Christians and churches are called and commissioned to take up whatever position on whatever socio-political spectrum, on whatever issue in whatever context, *that witnesses to and enfleshes in word and deed the concrete creaturely reality and relations that God has willed, decided, and enacted once for all in being for the creature, each and every one, in Jesus (through the Spirit), the last, first.*

---

1. For examples of what are often referred to as progressive-/post-evangelical views on this theme, see Wallis, *God's Politics*; Harper, *Republican . . . or Democrat*.

2. See, for example: "The gift of freedom, however, involves more than being offered one option among several . . . It is true that man's God-given freedom is choice, decision, act. But it is genuine choice; it is genuine decision and act in the right direction . . . When genuine human freedom is realized, inevitably the door to the 'right' opens and the door to the 'left' is shut . . . Human freedom as a gift of God does not allow for any vague choices between various possibilities" (Barth, "Gift of Freedom," 76–77).

I suggest that the particular *kind* of creaturely relations and commitments that God has willed, decided, and enacted in being with and for us all in Jesus (through the Spirit), the last, first, as glimpsed in Barth's theological vision, are more likely to land on the progressive side of currently available socio-political spectrums across a wide variety of socio-political issues. And this is the case *even though Barth himself does not land there on every issue.* Again, this does not mean that Barth believes there is something essentially better or superior about being what we call progressive in our current socio-political context, in the sense of some inherent, natural superiority to this identity. Barth's vision of free obedience to the claim and command of the Word of God is likely to show up on the progressive side of most ethical issues facing us today simply *and only* because this is what the creaturely relations decided for and enacted by God in being eternally, unequivocally, and irrevocably for us *all* in Jesus (through the Spirit), *the last, first,* happen to look like when fleshed out on the socio-political spectrums currently available to us. God wants *this* kind of creaturely life together: everyone shares what they have, so everyone has what they need; good news for the poor, the widow, orphan, and stranger. God does *not* want *that* kind of creaturely life together: the "haves" get even more while the "have nots" keep getting less; good news for Pharaoh, Herod, and Pilot. It just so happens that, in our contemporary historical contexts, the socio-political realities of the former (good news for the poor, widow, orphan, and stranger) happen to look more like what socio-political progressives tend to advocate for, and the latter (good news for Pharaoh, Herod, and Pilot) happens to look more like what socio-political conservatives tend to advocate for—again, only as these socio-political options happen to be inhabited on the current socio-political spectrums that happen to be available to us today for very particular, historically determined reasons.

In what follows, we will briefly look at a handful of ethical issues that press upon us with particular urgency in our time and place, especially in the context of the socio-political polarization between conservatives and progressives currently plaguing the USA, in particular, as that is the context in which and for which I write, but that is also in evidence in other nations and societies across the globe. *Sans* the safety and security of lists, rules, principles, or natural laws, we will consider what Barth's vision of free obedience to the divine command entailed in God's unqualifiable and irrevocable Yes to and for the creature in Jesus (through the Spirit), the last, first, might be calling us to in our time and place—a call that often places us beyond and even *against* Barth's own position on these issues.

ECONOMIC JUSTICE

The most obvious sign that Barth's theological vision and commitments can call Christians and churches to more progressive rather than conservative socio-political visions of the gospel, at least in the context of the West, is his own life-long affiliation with socialism. As we saw earlier, this left-leaning socio-political commitment was already in play early in his career, while pastoring a working-class congregation in a small factory town. Even before his post-war "turn to the Bible" and the full Christocentrism of his later theology, the Red Pastor of Safenwil already saw the biblical witness to Jesus moving in a different direction than liberal theology's identification with the so-called high culture and civilization of the West. Barth's early conviction: what the Jesus of the Bible was, wanted, and attained "was entirely a movement from below." Indeed, it was clear to Barth that the Jesus presented in the Gospels and at least the *idea* of socialism wanted the same things: "to help those who are least . . . to establish the kingdom of God upon the earth . . . to abolish self-seeking property . . . to make persons into comrades." So strong was the resonance, Barth could say that "*real* socialism is real Christianity in our time."[3]

While always critical of the failure of *actual* socialisms on the ground to be true to what the ideal of socialism *wanted*, as well as the way actual socialisms acted to achieve that ideal, Barth remained convinced that socialism—as a creative human vision of just social and economic ordering—constituted an albeit imperfect, broken "secular witness" to the gospel throughout his life.[4] This was particularly true given the primary concrete economic alternative on the ground in the modern world; namely, free market capitalism. If, for Barth, the God who *is* God wholly and only in their self-giving to and for the creature in the concrete history and person of Jesus (through the Spirit)—a poor Jew "from the lowest class of the Jewish people"; who "for his entire life with the exception of his last years . . . was a worker, not a pastor"; who "felt himself sent to the poor and the lowly" (as "one of the most certain facts we encounter in the gospel story")—then the concrete historical reality of Jesus's social location on the underside of history tells us something about who God

---

3. Barth, "Jesus and Social Justice," 36.
4. See, for example, Barth, *Dogmatics* IV/3, 114–35.

is and who *we* are called to be and what we are called to do in our creaturely lives together.⁵ In this light, one thing is clear for Barth, as I suggest it should be for all of us: what that creaturely life together might look like in any given time and place, including our own time and place, here and now, does not have private property, profit, competition, and inequitable distribution of capital at its center.

The point is *not* that socialism is identical with God's will lived out on earth as it is in heaven. Nothing could be further from the truth in light of how certain forms of socialism have played out concretely in totalitarian regimes capable of their own great violence and brutality.⁶ The point for us here is that socialism's vision of shared resources, universal solidarity, and interdependence appears significantly closer to God's will for creaturely life together than does capitalism's competitive vision of winners and losers where the deck is always stacked in favor of those already holding all the cards, i.e., already in possession of capital.

That said, we must remember the central thrust of Barth's ethics of free obedience: we are not called to simply hold to, conserve, and repeat past forms of creaturely life together—or to only discern and distinguish between currently available forms—in response to the divine Yes. We are also to enlist our creativity and imagination, our reason, curiosity, and aspiration. While inherited forms of socialism and capitalism remain the two primary global contenders for the socio-economic ordering of creaturely life together, they are not the only possibilities. There is currently a myriad of local experiments underway with various forms of alternative micro-economies, non-monetary barter economies, downwardly mobile intentional communities, all possible forms of free obedience to the divine Yes that takes up God's cause in the world—the last, first!—in *ad hoc* resistance to the dominant forces of private property, capital inequity, and profit. And there is nothing stopping us from imagining, creating, and inhabiting other as yet un-thought of possibilities for economic justice on earth as it is in heaven.

RACE AND WESTERN COLONIALISM

There are two key elements of Barth's theology that are especially relevant to determining Christian ethical responsibility in the face of the related realities

---

5. Barth, "Jesus and Social Justice," 23–24.

6. I am indebted to Weizhen Chen for "keeping me honest" on this point; for shining a light on my tendency to romanticize the socialist option, given the extent to which my own context as a citizen of the USA is determined by free-market capitalism and North American hegemony.

of Euro-centrism, Western colonialism and empire, racism and white supremacy: (a) the absolute rejection of any natural identity or even resonance between God and European culture that is entailed in his unequivocal no to natural theology; (b) his corresponding Christological commitment to the concreteness of God for us all in Jesus (through the Spirit), the last, first, as the content of the God-creature—and correspondingly, of the creature-creature—relation.

First, as we have seen, what Barth calls natural theology can be found in every kind of theology, every denominational tradition, and every ecclesial history, on both sides of the conservative-progressive divide: the positing of a natural (or supernatural) connection between the God and the creature that puts the former at the disposal of the latter, and thereby always places the neighbor in danger. However, the primary target of Barth's unwavering onslaught against what occurs in natural theology remained the liberal theology of modern Europe and its distinctive identification of natural human religious capacity and sensitivity with the divine. And at the heart of this identification of human religious capacity with the divine—the laboratory in which it was conceived, the soil in which it was grown, the test case given as its conclusive evidence—was the self-assessment of (so-called) civilized, cultured European *man* as the highest, fullest, and most superior example of the human being as such.

The dominos line up fairly easily and obviously from here. The primary target of Barth's scathing critique of liberal theology and of natural theology more generally was the civilized, cultured, religious man of Europe, in their self-aggrandizing self-assessment. The assumption that European civilization and culture, in their highest and most refined expressions, were the fullest and most superior expression—indeed, incarnation—of this natural connection between the human and the divine was inherent to this self-assessment: civilized European man and his culture took themselves to be the fulfillment of the incarnation of the divine on earth.[7] As J. Kameron Carter notes, this is "Western Man," as the "imperial God-Man," the central protagonist of and justification for the modern Anglo-European political projects of colonialism and empire.[8] As the presumed highest fulfillment and expression of the God-human relation, it is given into the hands of the Anglo-European imperial God-Man to possess the earth, to bring it under subjection and tutelage, or

---

7. For example, this is Hegel's philosophy in a nutshell. See Crites, "Gospel According to Hegel."

8. Carter, "Between Du Bois and Barth," 83ff. See also Jennings, "Another Knowledge of God."

so the logic goes. And it is this Anglo-European imperial God-Man who is and remains most directly in the crosshairs of Barth's theological polemics throughout his career.

Seen in this light, then, Barth's theology is—or *should* be—a direct attack on the heart of Western (European, British, American) colonialism, together with the racism of white supremacy that both drives it and was created to justify it. It is—or *should* be—then, a scathing attack upon the continuing histories of the church's complicity in and often explicit justification of Western colonialism and its racist violence, economic despoliation, and dehumanizing socio-political oppressions. Free obedience to the *true* God, for Barth, would then mean—or *should* mean—explicit rejection of the idol of the Anglo-European imperial God-Man, and the employment of all available creaturely creativity and responsibility in naming, analyzing, critiquing, resisting, and dismantling these histories and their complicities and structures while creating and sustaining just alternatives for creaturely life together in God, with and for each other, the last, first. For those of us who are categorized as white (meaning, let's face it, most of the people in any room of folks voluntarily gathering to read and discuss Barth, at least in the West), this means, of course, beginning with confession, repentance, and *reparations*.

I say *should* here, because both Barth and, even more so, Barthians—inasmuch as the latter can be identified as a particular theological species; a species, it must be said, within which I include myself—have been neither as clear and consistent nor as loud and strong as they could and should have been on these issues over the last century. Indeed, the norm has often been continuing robust complicity in, rather than faithful condemnation of and activism against, the Anglo-European imperial God-Man and his attendant structures and powers. Barth himself does not pursue the ethical implications of his theology for an explicit and sustained critique of Western colonialism to the extent called for by his own vision of the gospel. He can even employ the ubiquitous colonialist language of his day as if unaware of the performative contradiction he thereby enacts in relation to his own most thoroughgoing theological insights and convictions.

Second, as we have seen, the Christological concentration of Barth's "*only* in Jesus Christ" opens up and out into a universal embrace outside of which no one is lost (even by their own choice, weakness, confusion, fear, or failure). However, the concreteness of the Christological concentration means that this universal embrace does not occur everywhere and anywhere.

For Barth, the universal inclusion entailed in the "God for us all in Jesus (through the Spirit), the last, first," is no abstract concept of inclusion, no general universality. It is a concrete event that occurs *here*, and not *there*. That is what rankles progressive theological and ethical instincts. But what exactly does *here* mean in relation to Jesus? As we saw in Barth's relating of the Jesus movement to the ideals of socialism, it means *here*, on what liberation theologians call the underside of history, in the company of the poor, the oppressed, the outcast, the excluded.[9] And for Barth, as he says explicitly in one of his prison sermons, it means *here*, in the company of the "criminals crucified with him"—here, and nowhere else. We do not have Jesus, and so, for Barth, we do not have *God*, without "the criminals with him."[10] Or more accurately, God does not come among us, give Godself to us and claim us, in any other way, in any other company.

Again, Barth is not as consistent as he could be throughout the body of his work on this issue. And here lies the importance of consistently including "the last, first" in our rendering of Barth's vision of the Word of God that is God for us all in Jesus (through the Spirit). It is to constantly remind ourselves—*and Barth* (if he were still with us)—that the *all* can never refer to an abstract universality or inclusion, but is concretely actualized, once for all, in, by, and through a very particular *location* within, *ordering* of, and *way of inhabiting* material, enfleshed, creaturely relations: *the last, first!* Alas, Barth himself does not always specify the social, political, and economic dimensions of the material concreteness of the person, history, and reality of Jesus as the very particular way in which God is wholly with and for the creature. This leaves even generous readers of Barth like myself wishing he had been more consistent in specifying the particular way in which, in God, we are to be for each other as the last, first. His commitment to the particular concreteness of what occurs in *Jesus* (through the Spirit) certainly calls for it. But Barth often seems to fall back on a default view of Jesus's humanity as a humanity *in general*. And this generalized view of humanity opens the door for just the kind of abstraction that Barth is always targeting for critique and trying to resist. Further, we can now see what Barth could not or did not want to see in his own context: the default concept of humanity-in-general always means "white" humanity in Anglo-European contexts, determined as they are by the destructive fantasy of the imperial God-Man of Eurocentrism, racism, and white supremacy.

Relatedly, even when Barth is sufficiently concrete with regard to the specifics of Jesus's socio-political location, he does not sufficiently pursue the theological and ethical implications of the particular socio-political

---

9. See Gutierrez, *Theology of Liberation*.
10. Barth, "Criminals with Him!"

dimension of Jesus's humanity with regard to Western colonialism, race, and racism. For example, despite his affirmation that we only have Jesus—and so, God—in the company of those with whom he was crucified, he does not see how an innocent Jesus hanging on a tree at Golgotha reveals God's concrete solidarity with generations of innocent Black human beings hanging from lynching trees throughout the history of the USA, implications that James Cone and others have articulated with prophetic power.[11] Consequently, Barth does not see that Jesus's concrete humanity is expressed in what Cone calls Jesus's Blackness, both literally, as a constructed and imposed racialized identity based on skin color in the here and now of the USA, as well as in other colonial contexts; and symbolically, as that which is denigrated, demonized, marginalized, excluded, made vulnerable, and targeted for violence—yet is beautiful, blessed, and beloved of God in itself—in the here and now of *any and every* social, cultural, or national context.

Barth was regrettably limited in his ability to see and follow through on the radical theological and ethical implications of his commitment to the reality, history, event, and relation that is God for us all in Jesus (through the Spirit), the last, first, for the material realities of Eurocentrism, racism, and white supremacy. However, for those of us who have been and continue to be convicted and instructed by liberation theologies in our own time, there is nothing to keep us from following through on those implications with more consistency and greater depth. Yes, *all* are included in the concrete actuality of God's Yes. But that inclusion occurs *here*, at the manger, in marginalized community, on the cross, and *not* there: *not* in the emperor's palace, *not* in the corridors of power, *not* in the mighty chariot of war, *not* in the CEO's office with a golden parachute, *not* at the black-tie event in the swanky cultural arts center, *not* in the five-star hotels at the national meetings of the American Academy of Religion and the Society for Biblical Literature, *not* in the Hillsong megachurches favored by Hollywood celebrities.

There is nothing to keep us from seeing that the radical concreteness of Barth's "God for us all *only in Jesus* (through the Spirit)" means only *here*, among those who come last and count least in the established order of Anglo-European colonialism and empire: *only* in Jesus's poverty; *only* in his lack of legal citizenship status (as a middle-eastern person of color living in territory occupied by white, European empire); *only* in his marginalized economic and social status as homeless, as itinerant, as one who has nowhere to lay his head; *only* as a threat to the emperor's latest campaign to make Rome great again. If Barth's theology is taken seriously, free obedience to one's inclusion in the

---

11. Cone, *Cross and Lynching Tree*.

divine Yes to *all*, albeit *the last, first*, that occurs in Jesus (through the Spirit) can only put one directly in the crosshairs of any and all such campaigns of the empire, targeted as threat and enemy, by putting one in the company of and in solidarity with the widow, orphan, and stranger, the poor and oppressed, the imprisoned, the undocumented immigrant, the racialized minority, the trans and the gender fluid (more on this later), the persons with disability, the outcast—all those considered a threat to law and order, social well-being, and religious piety and purity by those in and with power.

In their own way, liberation theologies have also been much critiqued for being too particular and exclusionary. They are criticized for affirming a preferential option for the poor and oppressed that appears to exclude the rich and the privileged and the white from God's redemptive will and work—critiques just as often levied by white middle- and upper-class theological liberals as by conservative evangelicals. But in the words of the martyred archbishop of El Salvador, Oscar Romero, God's preferential option for the poor and the oppressed does not exclude anyone. *All* the rich, the privileged, and the white are invited to join God in solidarity with the poor and the oppressed—a concrete solidarity, of course, that can only mean the constructive dis-appropriation of their wealth and privilege toward the creative dismantling of the structures of poverty and oppression.[12] No one is turned away from that table. But your seat is at *that* table, and in *that* company, in the company of the poor, the immigrant, the leper, the prostitute, the tax collector, the criminal, the queer, the trans, in all the fullness and beauty of their God-created, God-willed, God-blessed, and God-loved creaturely humanity—that is, in the company of a Black Jesus.

GENDER

Gender and sexuality are two ethical issues in relation to which Barth's own specific positions must simply be rejected in the name of the unequivocal and unadulterated goodness of the news about Jesus (in the Spirit)—*for all; the last, first*—that he himself insists on at every turn. Yet even here, it is possible to argue that this can be done—and *must* be done—in the name of Barth's own fundamental theological moves and commitments. It is in relation to these two issues that Barth appears to clearly fall into the form of theological thinking that he himself claims to reject so strongly: natural theology. While

---

12. Romero, *Voice of the Voiceless*, 138. I am indebted to Paola Marquez for helping me see the necessity of making clear the (albeit creative and constructive) dis-appropriating consequences of concrete solidarity that are entailed for the rich and privileged, if and when they should ever genuinely seek to inhabit solidarity with the poor.

gender and sexuality are distinct though related issues, they are so intimately related in Barth's thinking that his irredeemable blindness on the latter is wholly rooted in his lapse of self-contradiction with regard to the former. We will therefore look at gender first and at greater length.

While the heart of the problem is Barth's lapse into the logic of natural theology, this lapse is not a straightforward matter. In fact, when Barth turns to the topic of gender in his doctrine of creation in the *Church Dogmatics*, he appears to reject the assumption that the nature and essence of gender is given in and with creation as a set of fixed, immutable characteristics—i.e., as a built in and fixed feature of our natural, metaphysical constitution—precisely on the grounds that such an assumption would constitute a form of natural theology. He scolds Emil Brunner for just this approach to gender.[13]

For Barth, the image of God in the human creature is not a fixed and static essence given in nature, a capacity possessed by the creature. Rather, it is a fundamentally relational action and event. It is enacted and performed as a concrete decision to be with and for the other, across difference. It is, in fact, nothing other than the creaturely act of free obedience to the divine command: be and live for God, and in God, be and live for each other, as the "other." And this goes for gender, as well. Gender roles are inhabited and performed as part of the creature's self-determination in response to free, living divine Word and action calling us to be with and for each other as the "other."[14] They are not essences dictated by nature. They are not immovably

13. This is from a passage directed at Brunner: "Thus it is the command of God itself which tells them what here and now is their male or female nature, and what they have to guard faithfully as such. As the divine command is itself free from the systematization by which man and woman seek to order and clarify their thoughts about their differentiation, so, in requiring fidelity, it frees man and woman from the self-imposed compulsion of such systematization. To what male or female nature must they both be true? Precisely to that to which they are summoned and engaged by the divine command—to that which it imposes upon them as it confronts them with its here-and-now requirement" (Barth, *Dogmatics* III/4, 152–53).

14. See, for example: "But what is the man in his sex and the woman in hers? When . . . it is . . . [a question] of ethics, and therefore of the command of God, we cannot and may not prejudge the issue with an abstract definition. Man and woman . . . summoned by Him . . . are in themselves as much and as little capable of description as the human individual in his particularity over against another . . . It is at the point where he is indefinable that he is sought and found by the divine command, that the decision is made, that he is obedient or disobedient, good or bad. It is here that man and woman affirm their sex or deny it . . . The summons to both man and woman to be true to themselves may take completely unforeseen forms right outside the systems in which we like to think. In no event is it bound to a scheme which we may presuppose. It is thus a mistake to attach oneself to any such scheme . . ." (Barth, *Dogmatics* III/4, 150–51). See also Sonderegger, "Barth and Feminism," 265ff.; Bodley-Dangelo, *Sexual Difference, Gender, and Agency*; Rogers, *Sexuality and the Christian Body*.

set in stone, existing in themselves apart from particular, concrete human responses to God's Word. In seeing gender as a creative act of creaturely relationality with and for otherness and difference that performs the image of God in creation through free obedience to the divine command, Barth provides all the theological grounds necessary for full affirmation of both gender equality and gender fluidity. So far so good.

The problem arises when Barth is either unable or unwilling to follow through on the ethical radicality of his own rejection of natural theology when it comes to the issue of gender. While unmooring the boat from the shore of nature and the natural on one end, he appears to be, at the same time, re-securing the boat to the shore on the other end. Barth re-secures the boat when he makes four fatal, interlocking, and *avoidable* moves that ultimately betray his own most fundamental theological commitments.[15]

First, Barth assumes gender as a fixed binary of two poles. *How* we inhabit those two poles in free obedience appears to be a matter of performative creaturely freedom, for Barth. To use our example in the previous chapter, Barth appears to allow that one's gender may be enacted freely in turning either left or right, *if* both directions are available options of performance and expression *within* the fixed location of *one pole* of the binary, i.e., within either male/masculine or female/feminine gender identity. One is *not* free to turn either left or right if that choice is a decision *between* the two poles of the binary, as if one was free to choose or change or move between genders, or as if there was a fluid creaturely space resisting and exceeding either of the two specified genders.

Barth is clear that these two poles are ontologically equal despite being different. He uses the example of the letters A and B as an illustration.[16] They are both letters, and so absolutely equal as letters. But they are two different letters, hence the binary. One possibility of this alphabetical illustration that Barth misses but that we don't have to: yes, gender can be creatively performed and inhabited differently, like the letters A and B are different, but there is no necessary reason—particularly if gender is not given in and dictated by nature—to limit the alphabetic representation to just A and B. There are, after all, a lot of letters in the alphabet; many more ways to be different in and as creaturely free obedience!

---

15. I am primarily indebted to Jaime Ronaldo Balboa's work on this material. See Balboa, "Slippery Slope." The pertinent material in Barth is found in "Man and Woman," in Barth, *Dogmatics* III/4, 116–240.

16. Barth, *Dogmatics* III/4, 168ff.

Second, Barth identifies this fixed gender binary of masculine and feminine with an equally fixed binary of sex identity: male and female.[17] In Barth's context, this has the effect of tying what is not given and fixed in nature—creatively performed relational and social roles of gender—to what apparently *is* given and fixed in nature: one's sex as either male or female. Today we are beginning to learn to question the assumption that a strict binary of sex identity is given and fixed in nature; to question the assumption that, while gender is culturally performed and enacted, one's sex is rooted in nature. However, the assumption that sex identity is naturally given and binary is still a powerful and prevalent habit of thought in our own time and place.

Third, Barth ultimately identifies the masculine/male with the social role of initiating and leading, and the feminine/female with the social role of responding and following.[18] And this is the fatal move that undermines his own affirmation of ontological gender *equality*. A and B re-enter the picture here. While A and B are both equal in their nature as letters, and so both equal in relation to each other ontologically, A comes first and B comes second. Correspondingly, for Barth, men lead and women follow. Even more, men are *created* to lead, women are *created* to follow. Here Barth takes what, with one hand, he insists are performative social roles, and, with the other hand, roots them firmly in the natural order of creation. (The extent to which one hand knew what the other hand was doing, in Barth's own mind, is an open question.) For Barth, this remains only a difference in social roles, not a difference of ontological inequality. But for us, we know this fixed identification of women with passive receptivity has, in fact, played out with the power

---

17. Balboa notes that this is related to a particularity of the German language that is not the case for English. There was only one word available to Barth for both gender and sex: *Geschlecht*. This linguistic constraint lends itself to—and perhaps informs—Barth's logic that gender arises out of the sex that is given in nature. Ergo, the root of his lapse into natural theology at this point, conceiving of gender as rooted in a binary of sex identity given in nature (Balboa, "Slippery Slope," 781ff).

18. See, for example: "For woman does not come short of man in any way, nor renounce her right, dignity and honour, nor make any surrender, when theoretically and practically she recognises that in order she is woman, and therefore B, and therefore behind and subordinate to man . . . She, too, has to realise that she is ordered, related and directed to man and has thus to follow the initiative which he must take . . . Properly speaking, the business of woman, her task and function, is to actualise the fellowship in which man can only precede her, stimulating, leading and inspiring" (Barth, *Dogmatics* IV/3, 171). If these passages were all that one read of Barth, there would be no reason to not physically throw the book across the room and never pick up Barth again or give his theology a second thought except as destructive enemy. One may still want to do that, of course, even after reading *all* of Barth.

and force of an ontological hierarchy, creating a virtually intractable social inequality throughout history.

Now, we may want to say that there is nothing inherently destructive in the particular relational differences of initiating/leading and responding/following. We all inhabit both of these social roles in varying ways, within the various relationships and in the various contexts in our lives. But it is the tying of these social roles to a static gender binary that is itself affixed to a static sex binary that does all the damage.

Fourth, the final stroke of Barth's problematic treatment of gender as part of human being in the image of God is the way he establishes gender difference—as conceived by the interlocking fixed binaries described above: masculine-male-initiating/feminine-female-responding—at the center of and as the very essence of human performance and enactment of the image of God. While we may want to affirm Barth's putting relation in, with, and across difference and otherness at the heart of the image of God and so of creaturely human being, it is the way he singles out the particular, presumed binary of *gender* difference as the central, primary mode of that relationality, and so of the image of God in creation, that is the problem. Again, on the basis of Barth's own no to natural theology, such a singling out of gender difference is wholly unnecessary and thoroughly avoidable. There are many ways in addition to how we inhabit and perform gender to be creatively in relation to creaturely difference and otherness as response to the divine command.

Barth makes these moves in the theological space opened up by his apparent rejection of any specific, fixed characteristics of human gender as given in and dictated by nature, in line with his no to natural theology. However, the cumulative effect of these moves nevertheless functions to produce the effects of natural theology: determining and fixing what is possible for creaturely human being in what we think we know about ourselves—i.e., in what appears to be a general anthropological knowledge and analysis of gender as a fixed binary tied to the apparently naturally given sexes of male and female—and *not* in the free, contingent event of the Word of God that is God for us all in Jesus (through the Spirit), the last, first, that calls forth creative creaturely response in free obedience. While Barth is prevented by his own limitations from affirming the performance of gender equality and fluidity as the ethical consequence of his theological vision—as free creaturely obedience to the divine command to be free for the other in love: for God, and in God, the neighbor, the last, first—nothing stops *us* from following through not only more consistently, but loudly and unequivocally, with precisely this affirmation.

SEXUALITY

As I mentioned above, Barth's view of sexuality—particularly same-sex relationships—is fatally rooted in his view of gender, as a logical consequence of that view. So here we will simply take note of that logical consequence and its lack of necessity in relation to and in contradiction of Barth's fundamental theological vision.[19]

While Barth's view of gender as a whole is at the root of his view of same-sex relationships, it is the fourth piece of Barth's view spelled out above that is central in preventing Barth from realizing the radical ethical consequences of his view (a) of who we are in the one Word of God that is God for us all in Jesus (through the Spirit), the last, first, and (b) of Christian ethics as free creaturely obedience to the divine command entailed in that Word, as these two themes relate to human sexuality. We have seen that Barth singles out and establishes a fixed gender binary of masculine-male/feminine-female as the central creaturely form of difference in and by which the human creature performs and lives out the image of God in creation, as the performance of intentional, responsible, and creative relation in, with, and across difference. Again, this bakes heterosexuality and heteronormativity into the very DNA of Barth's view of the image of God, and so of the human creature's expression of and obedience to God's creative and redemptive will, with all the inflexible force of natural theology.

The glaringly obvious consequence of Barth's absolutizing of a heteronormative and heterosexist gender binary in his theology of the image of God: same-sex loving relationships can never perform and live out the image of God or express the beauty and dignity of human creaturely relationality in obedience to God's creative and redemptive will. The only possible appraisal left open by Barth's view is that same-sex loving relationships are a creaturely aberration, a distortion, an illness, and, yes, a perversion. Regrettably, Barth employs forms of all of these harsh and all too familiar polemical characterizations.[20] Again, to characterize same-sex loving relationships in these terms is to define them as abnormal, as not natural, as against nature. And this is indistinguishable from traditional Christian homophobia grounded in natural theology.

Here, we simply need to point out again that there is nothing in Barth's theology of the one eternal Word of God that is God for us all in Jesus (through the Spirit), the last, first, that makes his particular view of

---

19. Balboa is also a key source for what I'm presenting here.

20. For example: corrupt, sickness, perversion, decadence, disintegration (Barth, *Dogmatics* III/4, 166).

gender—and so of sexuality—necessary or central. There is an inexhaustible number of possible concrete enactments of relation in, with, and across difference and otherness besides the equally inexhaustible ways in which human creatures perform and enact the particular differences of gender identity. This is especially the case if we ground our theological anthropology in Christology rather than in the biblical narratives of creation, as Barth insists we must. Last time I checked, the creaturely yes back to God that is enacted in the life and ministry of Jesus (in the Spirit), as the yes of creaturely obedience to the divine command enacted once, for all, does not include a heteronormative, cis-gendered marriage. In fact, Jesus's most intimate relationships are clearly lived out within a group of men, at least according to the Gospels.

All this to say, both gender and sex identity are certainly modes of inhabiting and expressing creaturely difference (in *multiple* ways!), but they are by no means the only or the central modes, if natural theology is truly and consistently to be rejected.

Finally, if Barth's no to natural theology is taken seriously, there is no more justification for singling out the social roles of initiating-leading and responding-following as the central and necessary ways of relating in, with, and across difference than there is for tying this particular relational difference to the difference of fixed binary gender and sex identities. Same-sex, gender fluid, and trans loving relationships are just as capable of expressing the relational difference of initiating-leading/responding-following so central to Barth's theology of the image of God as are heterosexual relationships, and in a myriad of ways. Indeed, one might be tempted to ironically and mischievously—but also quite seriously—*appropriate* Barth's view of initiating-leading/responding-following as a creaturely enactment of free obedience expressing the image of God in creation: What else can this view be but a robust theological affirmation and celebration of the corresponding roles of top and bottom often claimed and performed in gay relationships?

There is nothing in Barth's fundamental theological vision, determined as it is by the unequivocal Yes of God and the corresponding theological no to natural theology, that prevents us from inhabiting, affirming, and celebrating LGBTQIA+ identity, experience, and practice as full expressions of the image of God in creation—of relation with, to, and in an inexhaustible variety of differences—in free creaturely obedience to the divine command entailed in the great good news that God is for us all, the last, first, and that we are for God, and in God, for each other, the last, first; nothing, that is, except Barth's own inability or unwillingness to see and go there himself. Here again, we simply have to say our own *Nein!* to Barth on this issue, precisely on the basis of *his* infamous *Nein!* to Emil Brunner on the issue of natural theology, and so in line with his own most radical theological insight.

RELIGIOUS PLURALISM

There is one issue for which it seems clear that a case *cannot* be made for a progressive ethics rooted in the fundamental movements and commitments of Barth's theological vision. It concerns the status of religion and the religions. Barth's claim that God is for all *only* in Jesus Christ (through the Spirit), from and for all eternity, does indeed appear to be a form of absolute exclusion with regard to the status of religions as viable pathways to divinity. And if that is the case, there is no amount of theological gymnastics that could twist and turn Barth into a progressive religious pluralist.

It is true, there is no way Barth can be interpreted as a religious pluralist, at least not in the sense of a positive theological doctrine affirming all religions—or religion as such—as viable salvific pathways to divinity. And if this kind of positive doctrinal religious pluralism is taken to be essential to a progressive ethics, then here Barth can only remain a version of the conservative problem. However, while hopefully remaining this side of specious theological gymnastics, I believe it can be shown that Barth's relation to the issue of religious pluralism is significantly less straightforward than is usually assumed, such that the particular version of the conservative problem he represents is quite different from the conservative problem of religious exclusion as traditionally understood and inhabited. Indeed, Barth's version can be shown to entail its own strong critical judgment upon the traditional versions of Christian triumphalism, superiority, and exclusion that progressive religious pluralism means to critique and oppose, even as Barth cuts critically in the opposite direction with his own interrogation of the assumptions funding much positive doctrinal religious pluralism.

For starters, it could be said that Barth's theological vision entails its own qualified version of religious pluralism. For Barth, the gospel news of God's one eternal will, decision, Word, and act to be *only* with and for the creature in Jesus (through the Spirit), the last, first, is neither about, nor a work of, the human phenomenon of religion, much less the religion of Christianity as one of the "world religions." Though the church's witness to that concrete divine will, decision, Word, and action often can and does take place within the time and space—the historical, cultural, and material sphere—of what we, at least in the West, have come to call religion, it does not do so *necessarily*.[21]

21. See Garrett Green's new translation of—and insightful, reframing introduction

For Barth, Christians and churches are called to witness to the action that *God* has eternally willed and enacted on behalf of the creature and creation *apart from and prior to any and all human religious striving, questing, searching, desiring, or practicing*. There is an often overlooked dimension of this conviction: there is nothing entailed within it that prevents a celebration of what we call the world religions and human religious experience *on other grounds and in relation to other criteria*, for example, as valuable fonts of insight and wisdom into the depths and mysteries of human experience and aspiration, to which they can give powerful symbolic expression. Barth can be equally affirming and fully inclusive of all religions in this sense.

Further, there are two corollaries to this albeit qualified pluralist affirmation and inclusion. First, just as with so-called secular human work more generally, religions (including the Christian religion) are capable of functioning as *ad hoc* "parables of the kingdom," bearing witness to what creaturely life can look like as decided and determined in God's decision to be for us all in Jesus (through the Spirit), the last, first. And indeed, *non-Christian religions often provide this witness more frequently and faithfully than the Christian religion.* Second, just as God can choose, in God's freedom—most particularly, God's freedom from the *church*—to "speak to us through Russian Communism, a flute concerto, a blossoming shrub, or a dead dog," so too is God free to speak to us through the cultural traditions, practices, and artifacts of the world's religions (including the Christian religion). And as with the cases including a flute concerto or Communism, "we do well to listen to Him if He really does."[22]

For Barth, the so-called world religions, *including Christianity as a world religion*—indeed, religion as such—are *e*xcluded by God's eternal will,

---

to—a key passage of Barth's *Dogmatics* on religion: Barth, *On Religion*. This new translation has Barth able to say that—after and despite of all of Barth's familiar critiques and qualifiers of religion as a human phenomenon—Christianity is, or can become, "the true religion," in the event of concrete divine Word and action and faithful, free creaturely response. In his introduction, Green himself seems invested in this possibility for Christianity. I would want to argue with Barth himself, and/or with his translator, that a more faithful rendering of Barth's fundamental theological insights would say that Christianity can become "true religion"—*sans the definite article*—in the event of concrete divine action and faithful, free human response. The dropping of the definite article makes visible the possibility that Barth spends so much time across so many contexts arguing for: that God is free to act and speak outside what we understand to be "the church" at any given time and place, calling and creating the possibility for free creaturely response. If that divine acting and creaturely responding constitutes "true religion," than "true religion" can occur outside the church and so outside of "Christianity."

22. Barth, *Dogmatics* I/1, 55.

decision, and act to be for us all in Jesus (through the Spirit), the last, first, *only in the sense of being redeeming human pathways to God capable of connecting us salvifically to the true and living God according to their own natural resources, capacities, and powers.* Barth's theology, then, is not necessarily opposed to a general anthropological and/or sociological form of religious pluralism: it affirms there is a plurality of what we call religions; that this plurality includes a religion we call Christianity; that all religions are equally potential sources of human wisdom, insight, and symbolic expression of human experience and aspiration; and that all religions—*including the Christian religion*—are *equally incapable* of putting individuals, communities, or the world in redemptive relation to the true and living God as their natural, inherent capacity and possibility. This is simply the necessary methodological consequence of the gospel news that God has *already* given Godself fully and irrevocably *to all,* the last, first—whether non-religious, irreligious, or religious, whether heretical or pious in relation to whatever religion or non-religion—in the concrete, eternal-historical event that is God for us in Jesus (in the Spirit), the last, first, from before the foundations of the world.

As we have seen, for Barth, the good news of the gospel is not that *we* can find God, or that ultimate meaning is to be found in *our search* for God. The gospel moves radically in the opposite direction. The good news is that *God* has already searched for and found *us*, whether we like it or not, whether we want it or not, whether we know it or not, whether or not it ever occurs to us to search for God, and whether or not we decide to embark on that search if and when it does occur to us, and yea, even *before* any such search could or would ever occur to us—that is, "while we were yet sinners," as the saying goes.

Let's look more closely, then, at precisely what *is* excluded with regard to religion by Barth's understanding of the one eternal Word of God that is God for us all in Jesus (through the Spirit), the last, first.

As any good sociologist of religion will tell you, for all their potential for deep wisdom and insight into, and powerful symbolic expression of, the fundamental essences and boundaries of the human condition and the human experience, religions are *also—always*—institutional mobilizers of social, political, cultural, and economic forces functioning to order societies in ways that distribute power and resources toward some and away from others, privileging some and marginalizing others, rewarding some while punishing others.[23] For all the good they do, and they obviously can do a lot of good,

---

23. This sociological approach is primarily rooted in the work of Emile Durkheim; see especially Durkheim, *Forms of the Religious Life*. For a current and rather stringent version of this approach, see McCutcheon, *Critics, Not Caretakers*.

they *also, always,* function as powerful forces of social, political, cultural, and economic hierarchy and exclusion.

One fairly important thing, then, that is *excluded* by Barth's "God for us all in Jesus (through the Spirit), the last, first," is all the various and sundry ways that religions—*including the Christian religion*—exclude, hierarchize, marginalize, demonize, and denigrate not only practitioners of other religions, but certain communities of *their own* practitioners (e.g., women, queer folk, racialized or caste minorities). Whatever their relative gifts of wisdom and insight, every religion that assumes itself a pathway to God—or to the Ultimate, or to the Universal, or to ultimate Meaning, or to the peace of final release—entails some set of negative consequences both for those *not on* the pathway and for those on the pathway but *further down* or *further behind* on the pathway, those lagging behind, those not inhabiting or proceeding along the pathway correctly or consistently or sufficiently or committedly or swiftly enough.

While Barth's view of the "God for us all in Jesus (through the Spirit), the last, first," excludes *religion—including the Christian religion*—as a human pathway to the true and living God, *no practitioner or non-practitioner of any religion is excluded.* In Barth's view, the gospel is an *unconditional lover of creatures, and so of all creaturely practitioners—including bad practitioners, and even non-practitioners—of religion,* regardless of whatever religion is being practiced. It loves and embraces all practitioners and non-practitioners of any and all religions in active and overwhelming resistance to all the conditions, qualifications, burdens, and exclusions *religions themselves—including the Christian religion*—place on their own practitioners or with which they judge and condemn non-practitioners.

Finally, then, for a theologian like Barth, neither faith in the gospel, nor its theology (including Barth's theology), nor the church—*if and when they are faithful*—are permitted to violate, exploit, oppress, or harm those who are religiously or in any other way different from or "other" than the confessing Christian. For Barth, faith in and theology about the God who is unqualifiedly and irrevocably for us all in Jesus (through the Spirit), the last, first, commits Christians and churches just as unqualifiedly and irrevocably to the material well-being of the neighbor—of the "other"—in all their particularity and difference, including their religious or non-religious difference. This entails a commitment to reject every attempt to use religious or non-religious difference as justification for the mistreatment of the differently religious or non-religious neighbor, or for *any* treatment of that neighbor other than loving and responsible obligation to their material well-being—*including the defense of their religious freedom and identity, and the social, political, cultural, and economic status of that freedom and identity.*

At the end of the day, then, Barth does indeed remain wholly on *this* side of a positive theological doctrine of religious pluralism. However, in terms of a *socio-political* commitment to religious pluralism and a *theological* commitment to the practitioners (and non-practitioners) of all religions—while simultaneously holding religions, *including the Christian religion*, accountable to treat all practitioners and non-practitioners with justice, dignity, and equality: *the last, first!*—there *should be* very little difference in neighborly practice and behavior separating a theologically traditional person of faith who is thinking with a theologian like Barth from a good theological progressive. Alas, *should be* so often has very little to do with what actually *occurs* in the lives of Christians and churches.

ENVIRONMENTAL JUSTICE AND ECOLOGICAL SUSTAINABILITY

A theologically funded commitment to environmental justice and ecological sustainability is yet another area of progressive ethics that can appear hopelessly beyond the reach of Barth's theology, at least from the point of view of certain progressive theologies. This is because much progressive theological analysis of destructive human behavior in relation to creation sees an anthropocentric religious and theological vision as an inherent and irredeemable part of the problem. And Barth's theology does indeed appear to be inherently and irredeemably anthropocentric.

Progressive eco-theologies often see traditional theologies that put the God-human relation at the center of the God-creation relation as inevitably enabling or outright encouraging and promoting a human arrogance that demeans the value of creation while feeling entitled to despoil it in the name of insatiable human desire for profit, power, comfort, and convenience. At the very least, such theologies are believed to be incapable of providing enough incentive for the radical change in human behavior that is immediately necessary to avoid a cataclysmic planetary catastrophe. As *inherently* destructive to creation in these ways—according to this view—anthropocentric theological visions and confessions of faith must be rejected and replaced with a creation-centric vision and faith.

As regards traditional Christian theology and faith specifically, it is clear that belief in God's unique and uniquely salvific incarnation in the human being, Jesus of Nazareth, clearly places the human being at the center of God's redemptive concern, will, and action. This often results in the gospel story being told as a history between God and humanity, with creation and all its other creatures silent and mute in the background, if not erased from view, having no enduring place in God's eternal will, decision, Word, and action. Theologically, then, a commitment to environmental justice and ecological sustainability would seem to dictate that, at the very least, Jesus be displaced and relativized in God's redeeming and reconciling engagement with creation in favor of a more universal, planetary incarnate divine presence in, to, and for creation itself and for *all* of its creatures.

If things are indeed this cut and dried, then yes, Barth can only be a hopeless part of the problem. For there is no getting around the fact that his Christocentrism does place his theology within the ballpark of this kind of anthropocentric theological vision. However, it is possible to ask whether things are, in fact, this cut and dried.

First of all, does the centrality of the divine-human relationship that occurs in the divine-human event that is God for us all in Jesus (through the Spirit), the last, first, necessarily marginalize the rest of creation in an inherently destructive way? My provisional answer: not *necessarily*. Though it must immediately be said, loud and clear, that this is indeed how the centrality of Jesus to traditional understandings of the gospel has often played out in the theology and practice of the modern church, at least in the West. It is certainly how traditional faith and theology has been appropriated and used by maleficent capitalist forces—often flying the flag of a conservative Christianity—to and for their own ends: private property, possession, profit, power, greed, unlimited growth.

However, some recent sociological work on movements for environmental justice and ecological sustainability has shown that there are, for example, Christian evangelicals out there who make relatively traditional confessions of faith about the uniqueness and centrality of Jesus in God's redemptive engagement with creation, yet who, on the very basis of this explicitly anthropocentric—in terms of its being *Christo*centric—evangelical faith, engage in political and social activist practices for environmental justice and ecological sustainability.[24] What is more, as material practices go, some of these evangelical environmentalists and eco activists have been known to keep pace with committed theological progressives on this issue. This kind of sociological evidence alone suggests that, if the key issue is *ethical commitment, behavior, and practice* in relation to the natural world, a Christocentric and so

24. See, for example, Kearns, "Noah's Arc"; Smith and Globus Veldman, "Evangelical Environmentalists?"; Morris, "Young Evangelical Activists." For examples of work by evangelicals on environmentalism, eco justice, and eco activism, see the work of Cal DeWitt, Lauren Wilkinson, and Katherine Wilkinson.

anthropocentric faith does not *necessarily* issue in destructive behavior and practice or prevent constructive, activist commitment, behavior, and practice. The centrality of the divine-human relationship that is determined by a God who is unqualifiedly and irrevocably with and for the human creature in the material, creaturely reality of Jesus—Barth's own identification of Jesus not simply as human but as *creature* is pertinent, here[25]—can be interpreted to entail and be of a piece with an unequivocal and irrevocable divine commitment to and for the human creature's *habitat*: creation, the natural world. To love the creature *is* to love creation, for there is no creature apart from creation. This divine commitment is essential to God's parental care for the creature and God's will for creation as a whole. Correspondingly, the special status and role of humanity in this version of theological anthropocentrism issues in a special human *responsibility* for God's creation, as equally unequivocal and irrevocable as God's own commitment, not a special *permission* to abuse and despoil it.

Secondly, and specifically in relation to Barth's theological vision, Barth's *Christo*centrism is part and parcel of an even more radical *theo*centrism. A quick reminder: it is *God's* eternal Yes that is the first and last word determining all creaturely reality, comprehending it and setting its boundaries. Relatedly, everything is *from God*. Additionally, Jesus Christ (in the Spirit) is the center of the Trinitarian history that is the gospel story because of *God's* eternal will and decision, *as* God's eternal will and decision—and indeed, as *God's very self* in the flesh. This *theo*centrism displaces and relativizes even Jesus's humanity—*though it is by no means erased or negated*—in the divine-human reality and relation that occurs and becomes actual in the history and life of Jesus (through the Spirit). Indeed, rather than enabling or explicitly calling for human arrogance, Barth's theology is typically critiqued for being *too hard* on the human being, too relativizing and dismissive in relation to the priority of divine will, action, and initiative, for not empowering the human being *enough*—precisely by liberal and progressive theologies! In this light, Barth can only be said to engage in a very particular, qualified form of anthropocentrism.

Again, as we have seen, Barth sees this decentering of the human being that occurs in the fundamental moves and commitments of his theology as not only appropriate to the creature—rather than being unjustly and destructively diminishing—but as also issuing in a very specific, concrete naming, judging, and resisting of the very insatiable human desires that lie at the heart of human-caused ecological despoliation: the desire for power,

---

25. Barth, *Dogmatics* IV/2, 37.

for mastery and control, the desire to own, possess, and dominate. For Barth, this insatiable human desire is not only a theological problem—a desire to master and control the divine-human relation—it is also an ethical problem. It always spells bad news for the creaturely neighbor and for creation. What we have noted above about the strong prophetic critiques of capitalism and the imperial God-Man of the West implicit in Barth's theological vision are directly pertinent here.

However, this is where Barth's albeit qualified version of anthropocentrism does lead him—though not *necessarily*, I would argue—to curtail the not insignificant ethical resources for environmental and ecological commitments entailed in his own theological vision. Barth too often focuses on the theological and ethical dangers of human desire for power, possession, control, and domination for the *human* neighbor without sufficiently considering non-human creatures or creation itself. Barth most often speaks of the gospel as the history of "the commerce and communion between God and man."[26] It is here that Barth's theology needs to be instructed by both the concerns of eco-theologies and the new scientific research and data informing those theologies that has become available in the last half century, together with an awareness of the new and urgent historical context which that research and data make visible.

Properly instructed and responsibly aware of the dire dimensions of our new historical context vis-à-vis impending environmental catastrophe, there is nothing in Barth's radical theological critique of and resistance to the human desire for power, possession, control, and domination—the human desire to *place ourselves* at the center of all things—that prevents a full embrace of non-human creatures and creation itself as included in the category of the neighbor to, for, and with which Christians and churches are called to take up God's cause in the world, in free obedience to the divine command: be for God, and in God, for each other, the last, first! Seen in this light, it just might be possible that one does not, in fact, need to become a theological progressive in order to live and act as a responsible activist eco-warrior. It may be that one simply needs to obey the damn commandment: be caretakers, not assholes.

---

26. Barth, "Evangelical Theology," 11.

QUESTIONS

1. In what ways can the key themes and commitments of Barth's break with the liberal theology of the nineteenth century be seen to target the central assumptions of Western colonialism for critique?

2. How can Barth's no to natural theology be seen as theological ground for the affirmation of gender equality, gender fluidity, and trans identity?

3. Given Barth's view of the image of God, as intentionally enacted relation in, with, and across difference, name some ways in which we differ from each other *besides* the traditional, presumed binary of gender difference. How does Barth's view of gender require a pejorative judgment of same-sex loving relationships? How can this be seen to violate his theological rejection of all forms of natural theology? What would a Barthian *affirmation* of same-sex loving relationships look like?

4. How does Barth's "*only* in Jesus Christ (through the Spirit)" pre-empt a positive *theological* doctrine of religious pluralism, yet require what might be called an *ethical, socio-political* commitment to religious pluralism? Can you think of some concrete forms of practice and/or actions this latter commitment would take in your context?

5. How can Barth's *Christo*centrism be seen as a form of theological anthropocentrism that nevertheless functions to displace and resist the kinds of anthropocentrism (e.g., modern, neoliberal, consumerist, capitalist) that are most often identified as funding and justifying irresponsible, destructive human behavior in relation to the environment and the natural world?

BIBLIOGRAPHY

Aquinas, Thomas. *The Summa Theologica*, vol. 1. Translated by Fathers of the English Dominican Province. Notre Dame: Christian Classics, 1948.

Ariarajah, S. Wesley. *Not without My Neighbour: Issues in Interfaith Relations*. Geneva, CH: World Council of Churches Publications, 1999.

Augustine. *Answer to the Pelagians*, vol. IV: *To the Monks of Hadrumetum and Provence*. Edited by John E. Rotelle, O.S.A. Translated by Roland J. Teske, S.J. Works of Saint Augustine. New York: New City, 1999.

Balboa, Jaime Ronaldo. "'Church Dogmatics,' Natural Theology, and the Slippery Slope of 'Geschlecht': A Constructivist-Gay Liberationist Reading of Barth." *Journal of the American Academy of Religion* 66, no. 4 (Winter 1998) 771–90.

Barth, Karl. "The Authority and Significance of the Bible: Twelve Theses." In *God Here and Now*, 55–74. Translated by Paul M. van Buren. London: Routledge Classics, 2003.

———. "Christian Ethics." In *God Here and Now*, 105–114. Translated by Paul M. van Buren. London: Routledge Classics, 2003.

———. "The Christian Proclamation Here and Now." In *God Here and Now*, 1–12. Translated by Paul M. van Buren. London: Routledge Classics, 2003.

———. *Church Dogmatics*, vol. I, pt. 1. Edited by G.W. Bromiley and T.F. Torrance. Translated by G.W. Bromiley. 2nd ed. London: T&T Clark, 1975.

———. *Church Dogmatics*, vol. I, pt. 2. Edited by G.W. Bromiley and T.F. Torrance. Translated by G.T. Thomson and Harold Knight. Edinburgh: T&T Clark, 1956.

———. *Church Dogmatics*, vol. II, pt. 1. Edited by G.W. Bromiley and T.F. Torrance. Translated by T.H.L. Parker et al. Edinburgh: T&T Clark, 1997.

———. *Church Dogmatics*, vol. II, pt. 2. Edited by G.W. Bromiley and T.F. Torrance. Translated by G.W. Bromiley et al. London: T&T Clark International, 2004.

———. *Church Dogmatics*, vol. III, pt. 2. Edited by G.W. Bromiley and T.F. Torrance. Translated by Harold Knight et al. Edinburgh: T&T Clark, 1960.

———. *Church Dogmatics*, vol. III, pt. 4. Edited by G.W. Bromiley and T.F. Torrance. Translated by A.T. Mackay et al. Edinburgh: T&T Clark, 1961.

———. *Church Dogmatics*, vol. IV, pt. 1. Edited by G.W. Bromiley and T.F. Torrance. Translated by G.W. Bromiley. Edinburgh: T&T Clark, 1956.

———. *Church Dogmatics*, vol. IV, pt. 2. Edited by G.W. Bromiley and T.F. Torrance. Translated by G.W. Bromiley. Edinburgh: T&T Clark, 1958.

———. *Church Dogmatics*, vol. IV, pt. 3. Edited by G.W. Bromiley and T.F. Torrance. Translated by G.W. Bromiley. Edinburgh: T&T Clark, 1961.

———. "The Criminals with Him!" In *Deliverance to the Captives*, 75–84. Translated by Marguerite Wieser. New York: Harper and Row, 1961.
———. *The Epistle to the Romans*. Translated by Edwyn C. Hoskins. 6th ed. Oxford: Oxford University Press, 1968.
———. "Evangelical Theology in the Nineteenth Century." In *The Humanity of God*, 11–33. Translated by Thomas Weiser. Atlanta: John Knox, 1960.
———. "The Gift of Freedom: Foundation of Evangelical Ethics." In *The Humanity of God*, 69–96. Translated by John Newton Thomas and Thomas Weiser. Atlanta: John Knox, 1960.
———. *The Holy Spirit and the Christian Life: The Theological Basis of Ethics*. Translated by R. Birch Hoyle. Louisville: Westminster John Knox, 1993.
———. "The Humanity of God." In *The Humanity of God*, 37–65. Translated by John Newton Thomas. Atlanta: John Knox, 1960.
———. "Jesus Christ and the Movement for Social Justice." In *Karl Barth and Radical Politics*, edited and translated by George Hunsinger, 19–45. Philadelphia: Westminster, 1976.
———. *The Theology of Schleiermacher: Lectures at Göttingen, Winter Semester of 1923/24*. Edited by Dietrich Ritschl. Translated by Geoffrey W. Bromiley. Edinburgh: T&T Clark, 1982.
———. "Nein!" In *Natural Theology*, 65–128. Translated by Peter Fraenkel. London: Centenary, 1946.
———. *On Religion: The Revelation of God as the Sublimation of Religion*. Edited and translated by Garrett Green. London: Bloomsbury Academic, 2006.
———. "The Principle of Scripture and Its Grounds." In *The Theology of the Reformed Confessions*, 38–64. Translated by Darrell L. Guder and Judith J. Guder. Louisville: Westminster John Knox, 2002.
———. "The Proclamation of God's Free Grace." In *God Here and Now*, 34–54. Translated by Paul M. van Buren. London: Routledge Classics, 2003.
———. "Revelation." In *God in Action*, 3–19. Translated by Elmer G. Homrighausen and Karl J. Ernst. Manhasset, NY: Round Table, 1963.
———. "The Sovereignty of God's Word and the Decision of Faith." In *God Here and Now*, 13–33. Translated by Paul M. van Buren. London: Routledge Classics, 2003.
———. "Strange New World within the Bible." In *Word of God, Word of Man*, 28–50. Translated by Douglas Horton. New York: Harper & Row, 1957.
———. "The Word of God and the Task of Ministry." In *Word of God, Word of Man*, 183–217. Translated by Douglas Horton. New York: Harper & Row, 1957.
Berkouwer, G. C. *The Triumph of Grace in the Theology of Karl Barth: An Introduction and Critical Appraisal*. Grand Rapids: Eerdmans, 1956.
Biggar, Nigel. *The Hastening the Waits: Karl Barth's Ethics*. Oxford: Oxford University Press, 1993.
Bodley-Dangelo, Faye. *Sexual Difference, Gender, and Agency in Karl Barth's Church Dogmatics*. New York: Bloomsbury, 2019.
Boesel, Chris. "The Apophasis of Divine Freedom: Saving 'the Name' and the Neighbor from Human Mastery." In *Apophatic Bodies: Negative Theology, Incarnation, and Relationality*, edited by Chris Boesel and Catherine Keller, 307–28. New York: Fordham University Press, 2010.
———. "Better News Hath No Evangelical than This: Barth, Election, and the Recovery of the Gospel from Evangelicalism's Territorial Disputes." In *Karl Barth and the Future of*

Evangelical Theology, edited by Christian T. Collins Winn and John L. Drury, 162–90. Eugene, OR: Cascade, 2014.

———. *In Kierkegaard's Garden with the Poppy Blooms: Why Derrida Doesn't Read Kierkegaard When He Reads Kierkegaard*. Lanham: Fortress Academic, 2021.

Boesel, Chris, and Catherine Keller, eds. *Apophatic Bodies: Negative Theology, Incarnation, and Relationality*. Bronx: Fordham University Press, 2010.

Bolich, Gregory C. *Karl Barth and Evangelicalism*. Downers Grove: InterVarsity, 1980.

Brown Douglas, Kelly. *Sexuality and the Black Church: A Womanist Perspective*. Maryknoll: Orbis, 1999.

Busch, Eberhard. *The Great Passion: An Introduction to Karl Barth's Theology*. Edited by Darrell L Guder and Judith J. Guder. Translated by Geoffrey W. Bromiley. Grand Rapids: Eerdmans, 2004.

Capps, Walter H. *Religion: The Making of a Discipline*. Minneapolis: Augsburg Fortress, 1995.

Caputo, John D. *The Weakness of God: A Theology of the Event*. Bloomington: Indiana University Press, 2006.

Carter, J. Kameron. "Between W.E.B. Du Bois and Karl Barth: The Problem of Modern Political Theology." In *Race and Political Theology*, edited by Vincent Lloyd, 83–111. Stanford: Stanford University Press, 2012.

Clayton, Philip. "The God Who Is (Not) One: Of Elephants, Blind Men, and Disappearing Tigers." In *Divine Multiplicity: Trinities, Diversities, and the Nature of Relation*, edited by Chris Boesel and Wesley Ariarajah, 19–37. New York: Fordham University Press, 2014.

Collins Winn, Christian. *"Jesus Is Victor!": The Significance of the Blumhardts for the Theology of Karl Barth*. Eugene, OR: Pickwick, 2015.

Cone, James H. *The Cross and the Lynching Tree*. Maryknoll: Orbis, 2011.

———. *God of the Oppressed*. Rev. ed. Maryknoll: Orbis, 1997.

Cunningham, Mary Kathleen. "Karl Barth's Interpretation and Use of Ephesians 1:4 in His Doctrine of Election: An Essay in the Relation of Scripture and Theology." PhD dissertation, Yale University, 1988.

Crites, Stephen D. "The Gospel According to Hegel." *Journal of Religion* 46, no. 2 (1966) 246–63.

Dorrien, Gary. *Theology without Weapons: The Barthian Revolt in Modern Theology*. Louisville: Westminster John Knox, 2000.

Durkheim, Emile. *The Elementary Forms of the Religious Life*. Translated by Karen E. Fields. New York: Free Press, 1995.

Eckardt, A. Roy. *Elder and Younger Brothers: The Encounter of Jews and Christians*. New York: Scribner, 1967.

Elie, Paul. *The Life You Save May Be Your Own: An American Pilgrimage*. New York: Farrar, Straus and Giroux, 2003.

Gibson, Davie, and Daniel Strange, eds. *Engaging with Barth: Contemporary Evangelical Critiques*. New York: T&T Clark, 2008.

Green, Clifford, ed. *Karl Barth: Theologian of Freedom*. Making of Modern Theology. Minneapolis: Fortress, 1991.

Gutierrez, Gustavo. *A Theology of Liberation: History, Politics and Salvation*. Edited and translated by Sister Caridad Inda and John Eagleson. Rev. ed. Maryknoll: Orbis, 1988.

Harper, Lisa Sharon. *Evangelical =/= Republican . . . or Democrat*. New York: New Press, 2008.

Hunsinger, George, ed. *Karl Barth and Radical Politics*. Translated by George Hunsinger. Philadelphia: Westminster, 1976.

Hunsinger, George. *How to Read Karl Barth: The Shape of His Theology*. Oxford: Oxford University Press, 1991.

Jennings, Willie. "Another Knowledge of God Is Possible: Barth Among Post-Colonial Epistemologists." Princeton Theological Seminary's Annual Karl Barth Conference. Filmed July 2018. YouTube video, 49:27. https://www.youtube.com/watch?v=Kq2dixOGAwk.

Kant, Immanuel. "What Is Enlightenment?" In *Foundations of the Metaphysics of Morals*, 85–92. Translated by Lewis White Beck. Indianapolis: Bobbs-Merrill Company, 1959.

Kearns, Laurel. "Noah's Arc Goes to Washington: A Profile of Evangelical Environmentalism." *Social Compass* 44, no. 3 (1997) 349–66.

Keller, Catherine. *The Cloud of the Impossible: Negative Theology and Planetary Entanglement*. New York: Columbia University Press, 2014.

Littell, Franklin H. *The Crucifixion of the Jews: The Failure of Christians to Understand the Jewish Experience*. Macon: Mercer University Press, 1986.

Lowe, Walter. *Theology and Difference: The Wound of Reason*. Bloomington: Indiana University Press, 1993.

Luther, Martin. *The Freedom of the Christian*. Translated by Mark D. Tranvik. Minneapolis: Fortress, 2008.

McCormack, Bruce, L. *Karl Barth's Critically Realistic Dialectical Theology: Its Genesis and Development 1909–1936*. Oxford: Oxford University Press, 1995.

McCutcheon, Russell T. *Critics, Not Caretakers: Redescribing the Public Study of Religion*. Abany: State University of New York Press, 2001.

Migliore, Daniel L., ed. *Commanding Grace: Studies in Karl Barth's Ethics*. Grand Rapids: Eerdmans, 2010.

Morris, Alex. "For These Young Evangelical Activists, Facing the Climate Crisis Is an Act of Faith." *Rolling Stone*, March 21, 2021. https://www.rollingstone.com/culture/culture-features/young-evangelical-climate-change-activists-1144370/.

Perkins, Robert L. *Søren Kierkegaard*. Richmond: John Knox, 1969.

Reuther, Rosemary Radford. *Faith and Fratricide: The Theological Roots of Anti-Semitism*. New York: Seabury, 1974.

Robinson, James M., ed. "The Debate on the Critical Historical Method: Correspondence between Adolf von Harnack and Karl Barth." In *The Beginnings of Dialectic Theology*, 163–87. Translated by James M. Robinson. Richmond: John Knox, 1968.

Rogers, Eugene F., Jr. *Sexuality and the Christian Body: Finding Their Way into the Triune God*. Oxford: Blackwell, 1999.

Romero, Oscar. *Voice of the Voiceless: The Four Pastoral Letters and Other Statements*. Translated by Michael J. Walsh. Maryknoll: Orbis, 1985.

Schaeffer, Francis A. *How Should We Then Live?: The Rise and Decline of Western Thought and Culture*. L'Abri 50th ann. ed. Wheaton: Crossway, 2005.

Schwöbel, Christoph. "Theology." In *The Cambridge Companion to Karl Barth*, edited by John Webster, 17–36. Cambridge: Cambridge University Press, 2006.

Smart, James D., ed. *Revolutionary Theology in the Making: Barth-Thurneysen Correspondence, 1914–1925*. Translated by James D. Smart. Richmond: John Knox, 1964.

Smith, Amy Erica, and Robin Globus Veldman. "Evangelical Environmentalists? Evidence from Brazil." *Journal for the Scientific Study of Religion* 59, no. 2 (June 2020) 341–59.

Bibliography

Sonderegger, Katherine. "Barth and Feminism." In *The Cambridge Companion to Karl Barth*, edited by John Webster, 258–73. Cambridge: Cambridge University Press, 2000.

———. *That Jesus Christ Was Born a Jew: Karl Barth's "Doctrine of Israel."* University Park: Pennsylvania State University Press, 1992.

Tanner, Kathryn. *God and Creation in Christian Theology: Tyranny or Empowerment?* Minneapolis: Fortress, 2005.

Thorne, Philip R. *Evangelicalism and Karl Barth: His Reception and Influence in North American Evangelical Theology*. Allison Park: Pickwick, 1995.

Thornton, Max. "Cyborg Trans/Criptions: Gender, Disability, and the Image of God." PhD dissertation, Drew University, 2021.

Thurneysen, Eduard. *The Sermon on the Mount*. Translated by William Childs Robinson Sr., with James M. Robinson. Richmond: John Knox, 1964.

Tillich, Paul. *Systematic Theology*, vol. I. Chicago: University of Chicago Press, 1951.

Wallis, Jim. *God's Politics: Why the Right Gets It Wrong and the Left Doesn't Get It*. San Francisco: HarperCollins, 2005.

Ward, Graham. *Barth, Derrida, and the Language of Theology*. Cambridge: Cambridge University Press, 1995.